ZECHARIAH

GETTING BACK TO GOD

Study by Joey Clifton
Commentary by Judson Edwards

Free downloadable Teaching Guide for this study available at
NextSunday.com/teachingguides

NextSunday Resources
6316 Peake Road
Macon, Georgia 31210-3960
1-800-747-3016
©2018 by NextSunday Resources
All rights reserved.

TABLE OF CONTENTS

Zechariah: Getting Back to God

HOW TO USE THIS STUDY

NextSunday Resources Adult Bible Studies are designed to help adults study Scripture seriously within the context of the larger Christian tradition and, through that process, find their faith renewed, challenged, and strengthened. We study the Scriptures because we believe they affect our current lives in important ways. Each study contains the following three components:

Study Guide

Each study guide lesson is arranged in four movements:

Reflecting recalls a contemporary story, anecdote, example, or illustration to help us anticipate the session's relevance in our lives.

Studying is centered on giving the biblical material in-depth attention while often surrounding it with helpful insights from theology, ethics, church history, and other areas.

Understanding helps us find relevant connections between our lives and the biblical message.

What About Me? provides brief statements that help unite life issues with the meaning of the biblical text.

Commentary

Each study guide lesson is accompanied by an additional, in-depth commentary on the biblical material. Written by a different author than the study guide, each commentary gives the opportunity for learners to approach the Scripture text from a separate but complementary viewpoint.

Teaching Guide

In addition to the provided study guide and commentary, *NextSunday Resources* also provides a *free* downloadable teaching guide, available at NextSunday.com. Each teaching guide gives the teacher tools for focusing on the content of each study guide lesson through additional commentary and Bible background information. Through teacher helps and teaching options, each teaching guide also provides substance for variety and choice in the preparation of each lesson.

NextSunday
Resources

Study Introduction

The prophet Zechariah ministered during the late sixth century BC. His audience was composed of Jews who had recently returned from Babylonian captivity and were struggling to rebuild their nation under Persian rule.

This was a crucial turning point for the people of God. They stood on the threshold of a new beginning. Chastened by decades of exile, how would they use what they had learned about God, themselves, and covenant faithfulness to make a new way for themselves in their ancestral homeland?

Like the returning exiles, Christians today often feel led to restore their relationships with God and each other. Perhaps the lessons of Zechariah can help us in that task.

A VISION
OF PEACE

Zechariah 1:1-17

Central Question

What words of comfort do I long to hear from God?

Scripture

Zechariah 1:1-17 In the eighth month, in the second year of Darius, the word of the LORD came to the prophet Zechariah son of Berechiah son of Iddo, saying: 2 The LORD was very angry with your ancestors. 3 Therefore say to them, Thus says the LORD of hosts: Return to me, says the LORD of hosts, and I will return to you, says the LORD of hosts. 4 Do not be like your ancestors, to whom the former prophets proclaimed, "Thus says the LORD of hosts, Return from your evil ways and from your evil deeds." But they did not hear or heed me, says the LORD. 5 Your ancestors, where are they? And the prophets, do they live forever? 6 But my words and my statutes, which I commanded my servants the prophets, did they not overtake your ancestors? So they repented and said, "The LORD of hosts has dealt with us according to our ways and deeds, just as he planned to do." 7 On the twenty-fourth day of the eleventh month, the month of Shebat, in the second year of Darius, the word of the LORD came to the prophet Zechariah son of Berechiah son of Iddo; and Zechariah said, 8 In the night I saw a man riding on a red horse! He was standing among the myrtle trees in the glen; and behind him were red, sorrel, and white horses. 9 Then I said, "What are these, my lord?" The angel who talked with me said to me, "I will show you what they are." 10 So the man who was standing among the myrtle trees answered, "They are those whom the LORD has sent to patrol the earth." 11 Then they spoke to the angel of the LORD who was standing among the myrtle trees, "We have patrolled the earth, and lo, the whole earth remains at peace." 12 Then the angel of the LORD said, "O LORD of hosts, how long will you withhold mercy from Jerusalem and the cities of Judah, with which you have been angry these seventy years?" 13 Then the LORD replied with gracious and comforting words to the angel who talked with me. 14 So the angel who talked with me said to me, Proclaim this message: Thus says the LORD of hosts; I am very jealous for Jerusalem and for Zion. 15 And I am extremely angry with the nations that are at ease; for while I was only a little angry, they made the disaster worse. 16 Therefore, thus says the LORD, I have returned to Jerusalem with compassion; my house shall be built in it, says the LORD of hosts, and the measuring line shall be stretched out over Jerusalem. 17 Proclaim further: Thus says the LORD of hosts: My cities shall again overflow with prosperity; the LORD will again comfort Zion and again choose Jerusalem.

Reflecting

On a visit to an HIV/AIDS ministry in India, I had the opportunity to interview a young woman who had come for the first time. She told a horrific story of a near-death accident her husband suffered on his job. At the hospital, the doctors discovered he had AIDS and refused to give him care. Soon after, she discovered her husband had passed the disease on to her. With tears flowing down her cheeks, she described her difficult life. Because of the sins of her unfaithful husband, she faced shame, poverty, and the possibility of her own premature death. She worried about what would happen to her children when she and her husband died. Although she is a Christian woman, she admitted God didn't seem to be hearing her prayers. She wondered how much longer she had to suffer. My words to her were inadequate for all her pain, but I assured her that God did love her and understood her struggle.

Although the pain I have suffered in my life cannot compare to this woman's, there have been many low points when I wondered how much longer God would withhold divine grace. At each of these moments, when I turned to seek the divine Presence, I found God waiting to hear my confessions, to provide me with comfort, and to restore me to a place of faith and contentment. God seeks each of us, desires a relationship with us, and wants us to turn from our sin to find God. Even when life is going wrong, God does not abandon us. God is always ready to receive us.

Studying

In 539 BC, Cyrus, the emperor of Persia, issued an edict that released the Jewish captives from bondage and allowed them to return from exile. The first enthusiastic pilgrims who chose to return began the process of renewing their nation. They immediately set up the altar of burnt offering (Ezra 3:1-6) and started rebuilding the foundations of the temple (Ezra 5:16). Their success, however, was limited. The work was hard, enthusiasm faltered, quarrels with Samaritans arose, and several years of poor harvests

Cyrus the Great

followed. As a result, little was done beyond the temple foundations for the next eighteen years.

Then in the nineteenth year after Cyrus's edict (520 BC), the word of the Lord came to the prophet Zechariah (1:1) to encourage the people to resume their efforts to rebuild the temple. To Zechariah, the temple was a symbol of God's presence. It represented the renewal of the Jews as God's chosen people. His message to the Jews was not simply about the reconstruction of a building, however. Beneath that important task was an additional, more fundamental, calling: that of turning as a nation to God.

The word of the Lord that came to Zechariah contained both a call and a promise. If the people would return to God, God would return to them (1:3). Three times in verse 3, Zechariah emphasizes that these words are not his words but God's words. They are the heart of God's message to them through Zechariah. This is not merely a call to return to God's law or God's covenant. God says, "Return to *me*." It is a call to a personal relationship. Those hearing the words of Zechariah had an opportunity for a new future that promised the presence and blessing of God. They didn't have to be the "forgotten people" any longer; they could once again become the "chosen people" of God.

Zechariah pleaded with the people to learn from the mistakes of their ancestors, who hadn't listened to the prophets. He called on them to turn from their evil ways (1:4). Zechariah reminded his generation that though the prophets of old had passed away (1:5), God's words live forever and carry the power to overtake all who disobey them (1:6). The people respond positively to the prophet's call. Upon hearing his message, the people repent and say, "The LORD of hosts has dealt with us according to our ways and deeds, just as he planned to do." Sadly, this is the only place in the Minor Prophets that God's call enjoys a positive response. Elsewhere, the people's reaction is either ambiguous or explicitly negative.

Three months after the initial word of the Lord to Zechariah, God came to him again, this time through a vision. He saw a picturesque, peaceful scene among the myrtle trees in the glen. It was night, but he could make out a man upon a red horse. The vision unfolds gradually. At first, Zechariah only saw an indistinct horseman with other riders following him, each of a different color (v. 8). In verse 9, we learn more about this man's identity when he is called an "angel." By verse 11, we discover that this angel is in fact a being of some importance, for the other riders report to him. We then learn that this unnamed angel is, in fact, "the angel of the LORD."

> In Hebrew thought, words often carry the essence and character of the one who speaks them. Thus, the image of God's words overtaking someone was another way of saying God overtook that person.

As the riders appeared, an angel also appeared next to Zechariah. The prophet asked the obvious question: "What are these?" (1:9). Instead of responding directly to Zechariah's

question, however, the angel turned to the man on the red horse to get his answer. He learned that they were those whom the Lord had sent to patrol the earth (1:10), and they had come to report the whole earth was at peace (1:11).

That's good news, right? No, not to the Jewish nation, which was still living under the thumb of the great Persian Empire at the time. As long as the current peace continued, it meant that they were still a vassal state. Their dream for a reconstituted nation eluded them. On behalf of the people, the angel petitioned God, "How long will you withhold your mercy from Jerusalem?" (1:12).

Four horsemen riding horses of various colors also appear in Revelation 6:1-8. There, however, the horsemen are symbols of violence, death, and disease, not heralds of peace.

God responded to the angel with gracious words of comfort. Through the angel, God relayed his message of hope to Zechariah and instructed him to pass the message along to others. The message is this: God is jealous for Jerusalem and angry at the nations "at ease" that have made matters much worse than God intended (1:14-15). God has not forgotten the people. God promises the return of his compassion and the reestablishment of his home among them (1:16). God commits to rebuild Jerusalem, bring prosperity to the people, and comfort the nation (1:16-17).

It is appropriate that the Hebrew name "Zechariah" means "Yahweh has remembered" because God had not forgotten Judah. Zechariah's message to the people was clear: "Do not be discouraged because things are not happening the way you want or when you want. Do not doubt that God continues to watch over his people and bring comfort. God is still in control." When times are difficult for us, the vision of Zechariah reminds us that God sees, God understands, and God's compassion never fails.

In verse 17, the Hebrew word translated "overflow" has a more basic meaning of "scatter" or "shatter" that offers an additional interpretation. The verse could be rendered, "Even while my cities still have a shattered prosperity, the Lord will comfort Zion again and elect Jerusalem again."

Understanding

The words of God, "Return to me, and I will return to you," hold meaning for all of us. We can and should pursue the depths of these words for a lifetime. God deeply desires a personal relationship with each one of us. As in the days leading up to the exile, our sins destroy that relationship. Although the exile and devastation of Jerusalem is a telling example of what can happen when people refuse God's invitation, we don't have to look that far back in history. We only have to look around us at what the sin of our own world and our own lives has done to our relationship with God. Why are we so slow to learn from the mistakes of those who have gone before us? Why are we so slow to learn from our own mistakes?

Sometimes, even in our repentance, we continue to bear the consequences of past mistakes. At other times the turmoil around us is not even our fault. Life simply seems to be going wrong, and we want to cry out like the angel in Zechariah's vision, "How much longer must this go on?" When difficult life experiences continue indefinitely with no end in sight, we are often tempted to doubt the very existence of God.

The good news is that God hears our cries for help. God sees our repentance and our contrite hearts. God responds to our return to him by returning to us. God answers our pleas with gracious and comforting words that bring the promise of a restored relationship once again.

What About Me?

• *It is comforting to know that God desires a personal relationship with all of us.* Through his words to Zechariah, God makes it clear that God wants the people to return to him—not to a set of rules or rituals, but to a personal God. God wants us to know him personally, to live with and in God every day. Sometimes, in our sin, we wonder if God could possibly love us. The answer is an emphatic, "Yes!" Regardless of what we've done, God seeks us.

• *It is comforting to know that God does not give up on us.* Like the people of old, we are imperfect. We make mistakes, turn our backs on God at times, and act like we don't need God in our lives. Yet despite this arrogance, God continues to pursue us. God might discipline us as a loving parent disciplines a child, but God will not abandon us. God finds us worth restoring.

• *It is comforting to know that God understands our situation, no matter how difficult.* Life is hard, and having a relationship with God does not take our hardships away. Some of life's difficulties are the natural consequences of our own sins. At other times, the struggles are caused by other people or situations over which we have no control. Yet even when there seems to be no end to the turmoil, we have the promise that God sees and understands. God knows our situation and will enter it with us.

• *It is comforting to know that God promises restoration to those who seek God.* The Jews carried into exile admitted that they deserved what they got. They brought it on themselves. However, God makes it clear that restoration is the goal. We too must admit our mistakes and repent. If we return to God, God will return to us.

Resources

Kenneth L. Barker, "Zechariah," *The Expositor's Bible Commentary*, vol. 7, ed. Frank E. Gaebelein (Grand Rapids: Zondervan, 1985).

Peter C. Craigie, *Twelve Prophets*, vol. 2 (Philadelphia: Westminster, 1985).

James Nogalski, *The Book of the Twelve: Micah–Malachi*, Smyth & Helwys Bible Commentary (Macon GA: Smyth & Helwys, 2011).

D. Winton Thomas and Theodore Cuyler Speers, "The Book of Zechariah," *The Interpreter's Bible*, vol. 6 (Nashville: Abingdon, 1956).

John D. W. Watts, "Zechariah," *The Broadman Bible Commentary*, vol. 7 (Nashville: Broadman, 1972).

A VISION
OF PEACE

Zechariah 1:1-17

Introduction

As we begin this five-lesson study of the book of Zechariah, we
have the opportunity to delve into a book of the Bible that is
probably unfamiliar to many of us. Not only is it unfamiliar to
teachers, it is no doubt unfamiliar to those who are being taught
as well. That means we don't have to jump over the hurdle of
over-familiarity in this study. No one will be able to yawn and say,
"Been there, done that." A study of a book like Zechariah gives us
an opportunity to plow new ground.

When Zechariah wrote his book around 520 BC, the people of
Judah had recently returned from exile in Babylon. Under Darius I,
the Persian Empire now controlled the ancient world, and the
people of Judah were allowed to return to their homeland, albeit
as subjects of Persian rule. That homecoming, filled with antici-
pation, turned out to be a time of turmoil and uncertainty. When
the people got home, home wasn't what it used to be. The temple
in Jerusalem had been destroyed, jobs were scarce, familiar land-
marks were gone, and the old religious covenants were a distant
memory.

Into that breach stepped Zechariah and his contemporary,
Haggai, to offer a word of challenge and encouragement to these
people in transition. Zechariah's message to them can be summed
up in four statements:

• You don't have to be afraid anymore. You are entering a new era
of peace.
• You should rebuild the temple and, in the process, rebuild the
spiritual foundation of Judah.

• You should trust your leaders and see them as divine agents for good.
• You can be confident that God has forgiven your past sins and now lives among you to bring you blessing.

When you read those four statements, you can see why a study of Zechariah holds promise for us. Wouldn't we, too, like to shed our fear and be at peace? Wouldn't we, too, like to rebuild our spiritual foundation and get closer to God? Wouldn't we, too, like to trust those who lead us? And wouldn't we, too, like to bask in the forgiveness of God and know we are numbered among the blessed?

Those are the issues we will consider in this study. We begin this lesson by looking at the first seventeen verses in Zechariah. These verses focus our attention on a God who keeps coming to people in spite of their sin, a relentless God determined to have a relationship with people who don't deserve it.

The Lessons of History

"In the eighth month, in the second year of Darius," the book begins, "the word of the LORD came to the prophet Zechariah son of Berechiah son of Iddo" (1:1). The ministry of Zechariah lasted at least two years (520–518 BC). During that time he strengthened the faith of people shaken by long years away from home.

Zechariah definitely wrote the first eight chapters of the book, the chapters we will be studying. Chapters 9–14 were probably written later by an assortment of writers. Both the style and content of those final six chapters are different than the first eight chapters. They were almost certainly a later addition to the book.

The first eight chapters of Zechariah are filled with visions. In fact, they contain eight visions, each conveying a particular truth. But before Zechariah told the people of Judah about his visions, he reminded them of the lessons of their own history. In the first six verses of chapter 1, he reminds them about their ancestors, who had forsaken God and then suffered the painful consequences. He reminds them that those ancestors had eventually seen the error of their ways and repented and that they should do the same. Zechariah begins his book with the reminder that those who don't learn the lessons of history are destined to repeat them, and he doesn't want the returning exiles to walk the devastating path of their forefathers.

It has been said that the definition of insanity is doing the same things over and over again and expecting different results. Honesty demands that we admit that the people of Judah were not the only "insane" people in history. Most of us can look back at our own personal histories and see a little insanity there, too. Why do we keep forgetting God and going our own way? Why do we keep neglecting the significant people in our lives and giving our best time and effort elsewhere? Why do we keep falling back into the old habits that have hurt us in the past? Why do we keep spending money on things that don't satisfy? The questions can go on and on. Why do we keep living this insanity when we know better?

One of the most hopeful words in the Bible is the one Zechariah uses to open his book: repent. Repent means we can change. It means we don't have to keep repeating old mistakes. It means we can break out of old habits and open a new chapter. This was true for Judah after the exile, and it is true for us today.

God's Seven Encouraging Words

When Darius became emperor of Persia, he established an imperial post, a kind of Persian Pony Express designed to improve communication between the various parts of his empire. Zechariah's first vision—of patrollers riding on horses—may have been inspired by this innovation.

Zechariah saw a man riding a red horse. Behind him were other horsemen on red, sorrel, and white horses. They were patrolling the earth to see how things were going. They reported that "the whole earth remains at peace" (1:11).

This was actually bad news for Judah. It meant that Darius was firmly entrenched in power and that the Persians would probably rule Judah for a long time. Thus, the angel expresses what everyone must have been thinking: "O LORD of hosts, how long will you withhold mercy from Jerusalem and the cities of Judah, with which you have been angry these seventy years?" (1:12).

In other words, we've already served the Babylonians; must we now endure more humiliation at the hands of the Persians?

God's response offers the people of Judah words of encouragement:

(1) "I am very jealous for Jerusalem and for Zion" (1:14). God had not forgotten his people.
(2) "I am extremely angry with the nations that are at ease" (1:15). God was displeased with the Persians, the people at ease, and their harsh treatment of Judah.
(3) "I have returned to Jerusalem with compassion" (1:16). God had not forsaken his people and was with them in their pain.
(4) "My house shall be built in it" (1:16). The temple would be rebuilt and the spiritual center of Judah restored.
(5) "The measuring line shall be stretched out over Jerusalem" (1:16). God had Jerusalem in his sights and would restore its glory (see also 8:1-8, 20-23).
(6) "My cities shall again overflow with prosperity" (1:17). Better days are ahead, God promised.
(7) "The LORD will again comfort Zion and again choose Jerusalem" (1:17). Amazingly, God had sought out Judah again, chosen Judah again. In spite of her sin, Judah was the apple of God's eye, and God offered his comfort and forgiveness to the people.

When we get to the end of Zechariah's first vision, we find ourselves staring at the grace of God. Derelict, desperate people are affirmed and encouraged and offered a place at the divine table. Against all odds, the people of Judah have been chosen again as people God loves and is determined to bless.

Chosen against All Odds

Imagine, if you can, that you are in the fourth grade and playing in the neighborhood with your friends. Someone suggests a game of baseball, and teams must be chosen. Two captains are picked to do the choosing, and then the anxiety begins. Everyone wants to be one of the chosen. No one wants to be the last one picked.

You look down and toe the ground, lest anyone see the anxiety on your face. But then, wonder of wonders, the captain picks you first! Out of all of your friends, you're the first one chosen. You swell with pride and can't believe your good fortune. But once the game begins, your pride quickly becomes agony. As the first one chosen, you feel a certain amount of pressure to produce. The first time at bat, you strike out. Then on defense you let a grounder roll between your legs. The next time up, you strike out again. The harder you try, the worse it gets. When the game is over, you're devastated. You were the first one picked—and you blew it.

The next time the group gathers for a game, you know what to expect. After your last performance, you assume no one will want you on their team. The captains are chosen, and, once again, everyone starts toeing the ground. Then something incredible happens: you get picked first again! In spite of your strikeouts, in spite of your errors, in spite of your previous disaster, the captain wants you again!

Many of us can perhaps hearken back to our younger days and remember those pick-up games and the agony of hoping to be chosen. Only we remember the way it really was: after our first game disaster, no one wanted us. Begrudgingly, the captain took us on the team because we were the only one left. That's the way the world works—on the ball field, in the classroom, in the office, and just about everywhere else. Mess up one time, and you're dubbed a loser. In the real world, mistakes are lethal, and grace is in short supply.

But not in God's world. In God's world, we keep getting chosen in spite of our strikeouts, errors, and mistakes. In God's world, we hear the same seven things the people of Judah heard: I haven't forsaken you. I'm not happy with those who reject you. I am with you when you hurt. I want you to remember me and stay close to me. I know what's going on with you. I will help you open a new chapter in your life. I still pick you to be on my team.

Against all odds, God still chose Judah. And, against all odds, God keeps choosing us.

Conclusion

In the next lesson, we will explore Zechariah's final three visions. But for now, let's celebrate the main truth of this first vision. The people of Judah had been under Babylonia's thumb for seventy long years. They had come home defeated, depressed, and feeling like losers. In this first vision, God assures them of his continuing love. Yes, they looked to all the world like a ragtag bunch of homeless vagrants—but not to God. To God, they still looked like the chosen people, people capable of rebuilding the temple, people capable of restoring Judah to its former greatness.

Poet Frederick Langbridge once wrote, "Two men looked out from prison bars; one saw the mud; the other saw the stars." When God looked at those strugglers in Judah, he didn't see the mud; he saw the stars. And God used Zechariah and his strange visions to communicate his acceptance to those people. Zechariah had his visions, wrote them down for the people, and hoped they would catch fire around them.

Now, 2,500 years later, we gather in our churches to read his visions and try to make sense of them ourselves. It is not easy because we live in a very different world, and Zechariah's words seem strange to us.

It is possible, however, that once we interpret Zechariah's ancient visions, they will encourage us, just as they did the ancient Jews. It is possible that we'll read these old words to a straggling, struggling people and remember that, like them, God keeps choosing us.

Notes

Notes

2

A PURIFIED PEOPLE

Zechariah 5:1-6:8

Central Question

What must I remove from my life to experience God's peace?

Scripture

Zechariah 5:1–6:8 Again I looked up and saw a flying scroll.
2 And he said to me, "What do you see?" I answered, "I see a
flying scroll; its length is twenty cubits, and its width ten cubits."
3 Then he said to me, "This is the curse that goes out over the
face of the whole land; for everyone who steals shall be cut off
according to the writing on one side, and everyone who swears
falsely shall be cut off according to the writing on the other side.
4 I have sent it out, says the LORD of hosts, and it shall enter the
house of the thief, and the house of anyone who swears falsely by
my name; and it shall abide in that house and consume it, both
timber and stones." 5 Then the angel who talked with me came
forward and said to me, "Look up and see what this is that is
coming out." 6 I said, "What is it?" He said, "This is a basket
coming out." And he said, "This is their iniquity in all the land."
7 Then a leaden cover was lifted, and there was a woman sitting
in the basket! 8 And he said, "This is Wickedness." So he thrust
her back into the basket, and pressed the leaden weight down on
its mouth. 9 Then I looked up and saw two women coming
forward. The wind was in their wings; they had wings like the
wings of a stork, and they lifted up the basket between earth and
sky. 10 Then I said to the angel who talked with me, "Where are
they taking the basket?" 11 He said to me, "To the land of

Shinar, to build a house for it; and when this is prepared, they will set the basket down there on its base." 6:1 And again I looked up and saw four chariots coming out from between two mountains—mountains of bronze. 2 The first chariot had red horses, the second chariot black horses, 3 the third chariot white horses, and the fourth chariot dappled gray horses. 4 Then I said to the angel who talked with me, "What are these, my lord?" 5 The angel answered me, "These are the four winds of heaven going out, after presenting themselves before the LORD of all the earth. 6 The chariot with the black horses goes toward the north country, the white ones go toward the west country, and the dappled ones go toward the south country." 7 When the steeds came out, they were impatient to get off and patrol the earth. And he said, "Go, patrol the earth." So they patrolled the earth. 8 Then he cried out to me, "Lo, those who go toward the north country have set my spirit at rest in the north country."

Reflecting

My wife and I took a vacation to Gulf Shores, Alabama, where they hold the annual National Shrimp Festival. As well as enjoying the food, activities, and music of the festival, we found ourselves, along with our friends, spending a good deal of time on the balcony of our room looking at the beach. During the day, a small airplane regularly circled the area. Approximately every half hour, it flew parallel to the beach for several miles before turning and making the loop once again. Behind the plane trailed a long banner advertising a local business. Usually it displayed something like "Mel's Shrimp Shack" or "Betty's Dive Shop" along with a phone number or address. The implication was, of course, that Mel had great shrimp, and if you wanted to go diving, Betty was the best person to see.

As I studied this passage from Zechariah, I began to wonder how a more negative banner might be received. For example, what if the message trailing behind the plane read, "The Judgment is coming. Are you ready?" or "You are a sinner. Repent!" Occasionally, we see such messages on billboards or placards carried by street preachers. The most common reaction to such a sign is to ignore it. We see no benefit to us in that type of message. But this is exactly the kind of banner God shows Zechariah. In this lesson, we discover that there is real benefit for those who take the call to repentance and righteousness seriously.

Studying

Last lesson we learned that the Israelites lamented the peace that existed because it meant they were still dominated by Persia. While external peace existed in the lack of conflict between nations, inner peace escaped them. True peace, peace that lives within us, comes as the result of repentance and the elimination of our sin. In this passage, God gives Zechariah three visions in a row to punctuate the importance of this truth.

In the first vision, Zechariah looks up to see a huge scroll, thirty feet wide and fifteen feet high, floating in the sky (5:1-2). The scroll is so large that no one can miss it. On one side of the banner is a curse that says, "Everyone who steals shall be cut off." On the other side is another curse: "Everyone who swears falsely shall be cut off" (5:3). The scroll is making its way to every home in the land where sin abounds, bringing condemnation and destruction to those who live there (5:4).

"Do not lie" and "do not steal" may have been two of the commandments most transgressed in Zechariah's day. Thus, in verse 3 God pointed Zechariah and the people back to the original covenant on which they were to build the foundation of their lives (Ex 20:15-16). They could build the foundation of the temple all they wanted, but unless their own lives were built on obedience to God, everything else was useless. A nation built on lying, stealing, and irreverence toward God cannot stand.

In the second vision, Zechariah sees a basket used for carrying and measuring grain. Beneath the leaden cover on the basket is a woman who represents the essence of wickedness (5:7-8). Two winged women lift up the basket with all its wickedness and take it to the land of Shinar (5:9-11). Many scholars believe Shinar is a synonym for Babylon. If this is true, God is sending Judah's sin to the land of their enemy, where the people idolize wickedness. The message seems to be that wickedness will have no place in Israel in the future. It must be pushed back into the basket (5:8) so that it won't spread its evil across the nation. It must be removed to a distant land where the people do not know God.

An ephah was a grain measure. Although we don't know exactly how large it was, estimates put it at about 40 liters or half a bushel. The ephah mentioned in Zechariah 5:6 would have been a basket of about this size.

In this vision, God moves beyond individual sins to address the widespread wickedness that had covered the land and everyone in it. God's concern is the inclination toward sin that filled the hearts and lives of the people living in Judah. God wants the wickedness that lies within us to be sealed up and permanently removed.

When wickedness tries to escape, the angel (with some effort) thrusts it back in place. Wickedness continuously tries to find its way into our land and our lives. It is easy for us to think we have our sin under control. In reality, we never do. The only way to free ourselves from sin is to remove it permanently. In this vision, God's angel forces wickedness back into the basket, and God's winged creatures carry it away. Ultimately, only God can remove sin. God has provided a way to do that through Christ's death. The sacrifice of Jesus removes the guilt of our sin completely.

Zechariah's last vision in 6:1-8 reminds us of his first with the horses of different colors that patrol the earth (1:8-11). It paints a picture of God's great power over all things. God is referred to as the "LORD of all the earth" (6:5). The Babylonians and Persians may have thought they were in control of the vast empires of the world, but in reality it was always God. As the inhabitants of Judah rebuilt the temple and a place for God to call "home," they were not to forget that God is not confined to one place nor one nation. God is God over all things and cannot be limited by the finite minds of humankind.

The horses and chariots are sent to patrol the entire earth. Those that go north to the land of Babylon "set [God's] spirit at rest" (6:8). To "set at rest" here means to "light upon, descend, or settle upon." The verse doesn't tell us what the spirit will do when it settles upon the land. Presumably, it is an image of judgment

as God's spirit descends upon those who sinned against God's people.

Understanding

The hearts and minds of those rebuilding the temple were focused on national autonomy. They hoped for the reestablishment of their nation. They saw the temple as crucial to that goal. The temple was a statement that God was on their side. God's message through Zechariah, however, made it clear that the temple was not enough. What God really wanted was a restored relationship that could come only with the removal of sin. How could they continue to do the "work of God" by rebuilding the temple and simultaneously cheat or steal from their neighbors? How could they continue to bear false witness or lie about their neighbors? How could they continue to ignore and distort the law of God for their own purposes? God's answer was that they couldn't. The tendency toward sin had to be removed from their lives if they were to have any hope for peace and prosperity.

Centuries later, this message is still true. Too often, Christians get so caught up in "building" their churches—whether the number of people or the grand physical structures—that they miss the more important part, the building of righteousness in our lives.

The first step to developing righteousness is to identify our sins. Are we personally guilty of stealing, lying, or some other transgression? All of us are guilty to some degree and are called to repent. More fundamentally, however, we must come to terms with the fact that we all have an inclination toward sin. Everyone sins and falls short of the glory of God (Rom 3:23). God desires to remove that sin from us. Thankfully, God has provided a way to do this through the death, burial, and resurrection of Jesus Christ. He has done for us what we could not do for ourselves.

> How can we encourage each other to confront specific issues and work to remove them from our lives? What is God's role in this process?

What About Me?

• *How do you seek peace for your life?* It is easy for us to seek personal peace in activities, worldly pleasures, or even religious activity, hoping that God might reward us with peace for our efforts on

God's behalf. True peace, however, comes only through a right relationship with God.

• *When you are honest with yourself, what sins can you identify in your life?* All of us deal with sins. Some of these are ongoing habits; others creep up on us suddenly. Regardless, we must be honest with ourselves about the ways in which our lives fall short of God's glory. Confession and repentance restore our relationship with God.

• *How do we help others see their sin and wickedness?* Zechariah shared his visions with the people in order to point out their sins. In our society, we are often reluctant to point out sins. This is because we are well aware of our own failures and because our individualistic world tells us that the sins of another are none of our business. Nevertheless, in the body of Christ we are accountable to one another both to point out sin and to repent of sin for the common good.

• *Is it possible to contain wickedness and remove it from our world?* Although it is important for us to recognize our sin and repent, none of us are able to remove sin completely from our lives apart from the grace offered to us through Jesus Christ. Ultimately, only God can cleanse us of our sin.

• *How do we help the world understand the cost of sinfulness?* For Judah, wickedness threatened to destroy any hope for the future. The same is true for us. Political battles are fought constantly around the world, but the only hope for peace between nations and for every human being comes in the battle against wickedness. What can believers do to help people understand the seriousness of sin?

Resources

Kenneth L. Barker, "Zechariah," *The Expositor's Bible Commentary*, vol. 7, ed. Frank E. Gaebelein (Grand Rapids: Zondervan, 1985).

Chad Brand and Charles Draper, eds., *Holman Illustrated Bible Dictionary* (Nashville: Holman, 2003).

Peter C. Craigie, *Twelve Prophets*, vol. 2 (Philadelphia: Westminster, 1985).

D. Winton Thomas and Theodore Cuyler Speers, "The Book of Zechariah," *The Interpreter's Bible*, vol. 6 (Nashville: Abingdon, 1956).

John D. W. Watts, "Zechariah," *The Broadman Bible Commentary*, vol. 7 (Nashville: Broadman, 1972).

A PURIFIED
PEOPLE
Zechariah 5:1-6:8

Introduction

When Zechariah wrote his prophecy around 520 BC, he had one
primary purpose. He wanted to spark a spiritual revival in Judah,
and he thought that could best be accomplished if the people
would focus on rebuilding the temple in Jerusalem. Both
Zechariah and Haggai saw rebuilding the temple as a way to
rebuild the spiritual fabric of the people of Judah.

In a series of eight visions, Zechariah tried to stoke the spiritual fire among those who had returned from Babylonian
captivity. Imagine, for a moment, how it must have been for
those returning exiles. For fifty years, they had been away from
home. But they had also been away from the temple, away from
their significant rituals and symbols, and away from a regular
time of worship among family and friends. For fifty long years,
they had been in a different culture where their God was
unknown.

No wonder Zechariah saw rebuilding the temple as the key to
their renewal. If only they had a place—a center, a symbol of the
true and living God—the whole nation would remember God and
experience revival. As they rebuilt the temple, they would remember who they were and what they had always believed.

In the last lesson, we looked at the opening verses of the book,
which included the first vision of Zechariah. It was a vision of
four horsemen patrolling the earth, and it gave God opportunity
to speak words of encouragement to the people of Judah. That
vision was followed by a succession of others:

The Second Vision: Four Horses and Four Blacksmiths (1:18-21). This vision suggested that Judah's hope against the nations of the world was tied not to military might but to rebuilding the temple and reestablishing its relationship to God.

The Third Vision: the Man with the Measuring Line (2:1-13). This vision was directed to those still in exile in Babylon, encouraging them to come home and embrace a good future.

The Fourth Vision: the High Priest in the Heavenly Court (3:1-10). This vision affirmed the ministry of Joshua, the high priest of Judah.

The Fifth Vision: the Lampstand and the Olive Trees (4:1-14). This vision affirmed the leadership of Zerubbabel, the governor of Judah.

Our focal passage for this lesson gives us the final three visions of Zechariah. As he continued his attempt to stir spiritual renewal among those discouraged people, he offered them three more arresting images.

The Final Three Visions

The Sixth Vision: the Flying Scroll (5:1-4). Zechariah saw a gigantic flying scroll, approximately thirty feet by fifteen feet. This scroll was inscribed with God's curse upon sinners, and it patrolled the land of Judah. When the scroll detected the sins of stealing and lying, it descended upon that house and destroyed it.

Any of the exiles who had forgotten the strong demands of God would have been reminded that the standards had not been erased while they were in exile. This vision was a reminder to the people that they were holy and set apart. God expected a lot of them. Zechariah's vision called them to repent.

The Seventh Vision: the Flying Basket (5:5-11). Next, Zechariah saw a huge basket ready to take flight from Judah. When he looked in the basket, he discovered a woman there. This woman represented all of the wickedness in the land. Two other women, with the wings of a stork, appeared and flew the basket to Shinar, the ancient name for Babylon. In Shinar, a temple was erected to the evil in the basket, implying that the religion of Babylon was anything but godly.

This vision, too, was a call to repentance. The people of Judah were to flee wickedness, get rid of any remnants of Babylonian paganism they might have picked up during their exile, and return to God.

The Eighth Vision: the Four Chariots (6:1-8). This vision is reminiscent of the first vision we studied last lesson. In this final vision, Zechariah again saw colorful horses, only in this one they are pulling chariots. As in the first vision, these horses and their drivers patrol the earth so they can bring a report to the Lord. The report they bring is this: "Lo, those who go toward the north country have set my spirit at rest in the north country" (6:8).

This report might well mean that God is pleased that those left in Babylon (the north country) have decided to come home. Or it might mean that God is pleased that those in the north country of Babylon have been conquered and will inflict no more pain on Judah. Whatever it means, it offered hope to those returning exiles. There was good news from "up north," and the people could trust the sovereignty of God over world affairs.

When we look at these final three visions, we see the two main emphases in the book of Zechariah, and, it could be argued, the two main emphases in the Bible as a whole: repentance and faith. Visions six and seven called the people to change their ways, to take charge of their relationship with God and repent. The final vision, along with the first one we looked at last lesson, called the people to trust God, to know that God is sovereign over their lives.

Those two emphases seem to be at odds, though. Does spiritual renewal depend on our efforts or on God's? Do we have to work hard to come alive spiritually or simply lean into God's sovereignty? Which way leads to revival: repentance or faith? Let's spend a moment probing these seemingly contradictory ideas.

Addition by Subtraction

Zechariah consistently called the people of Judah to repent. They were to quit stealing and lying. They were to get rid of any wickedness in the land. They were to remember the sins of their forefathers and learn the painful lessons of history. In short,

Zechariah emphasized what many other biblical writers do; that is, in order to move ahead spiritually, we have to get rid of some things. The only way to add freshness and vitality to our walk with God is to subtract sin from our lives. On a journey with God, addition comes only by subtraction.

There is an old story about a man who complained every day about his lunch. Every day his coworkers would have to listen to a diatribe about the lousy meal in his paper sack. He wished he could have something besides a stale sandwich. He longed for the kind of lunches some of his coworkers had. He was sick and tired of getting the same stuff day after day. Finally, one coworker could take his griping no longer.

"Why don't you quit complaining about your lunch and do something about it? Why don't you tell whomever is packing your lunch to give you something different? And who packs your lunch anyway?"

"I do," the man said sheepishly.

The truth is, we all pack our own lunch. The law of sowing and reaping hasn't been repealed. We still reap what we sow, so we would do well to monitor our sowing. That was the message of Zechariah to those ancient Jews, and it is the recurring message of the biblical writers to us. We all pack our own lunch. We all reap what we sow. We all suffer the consequences of our sins and the blessings of our virtues.

We can't read Zechariah without at least asking ourselves what we need to subtract from our lives. If not stealing and lying, the sins mentioned in the sixth vision, what are our sins? Greed? Lust? Apathy? Anger? What do we need to subtract from our lives so that our relationship with God can blossom?

Leaning into God

The second emphasis in Zechariah is faith. Yes, the people of Judah were to repent of their sins. But they were also to lean into the sovereignty of God. God was working in the world, even up in "the north country," and the people were to trust that God was in control.

Zechariah was calling the people of Judah to be responsible for what they could control (repentance) and to trust God for what they couldn't control (faith). Some things are within our sphere of control. We can control our stealing, lying, and other personal sins. In fact, no one but us can control those sins. When it comes to much of what happens to us and within us, we do pack our own lunch.

But let's face it: most of what happens in the world, and much of what happens to us personally, is beyond our power. We have little control over what happens in "the north country" and have to trust the sovereignty of God. Consistently in Scripture, that is what we are called to do. We are to trust God when we read the awful news in the morning newspaper. We are to trust God when things in our own lives—sickness, accidents, catastrophes—suddenly invade our serenity. When we are confronted with issues beyond our own power, we are to trust the goodness of God. When we can't control what happens, we can at least trust that a good and loving God is sovereign.

That truth became crystal clear some 550 years after Zechariah. Jesus came into the world, died on a Roman cross, and then, amazingly, walked out of the tomb and defeated death. According to the New Testament writers, those events secured our right standing with God. When it comes to our relationship with God, none of us can pack our own lunch. God has already packed it for us. Our part is to celebrate that and lean into God's goodness. Zechariah didn't know about the cross and resurrection, but he did know that the people of Judah could trust the goodness of their God.

As Zechariah says in chapter 4 when encouraging Zerubbabel to get on with rebuilding the temple, "Not by might, nor by power, but by my spirit, says the Lord of hosts" (4:6). For sure, the people of Judah would have to put "sweat equity" into the temple, but they would also have to trust God. That project was too big for human effort alone. They would need the spirit of God working within and among them to accomplish that task.

Conclusion

Zechariah's sixth and seventh visions are about repentance. His final vision doesn't allude to repentance at all but reminds the people that God is alive and well and working in the world. So, which is it? Repentance or faith? Did the people of Judah need to do something themselves or simply trust God to do something?

Well, let's seek New Testament help in answering those questions. Let's ask Paul about it. Is it our works, our repentance, that gives us spiritual renewal? "For by grace you have been saved through faith, and this is not your own doing; it is the gift of God—not the result of works, so that no one may boast" (Eph 2:8-9). So, there's our answer from Paul. It's all of God. Renewal is God's gift to us.

Shall we then do nothing? Shall we never work, sweat, or change? "For we are what he has made us, created in Christ Jesus for good works, which God prepared beforehand to be our way of life" (Eph 2:10). So, there's Paul's answer to this question. Our way of life is to be one of good works: a way of work, sweat, and change.

The only conclusion we can draw from the biblical witness is that spiritual renewal is a paradox. It comes only when we work as if it all depends on our effort and have faith as if it all depends on God's effort. The Christian dance is a two-step: the gracious, sustaining spirit of God and our response of repentance borne of gratitude.

Spiritual vitality is not "either-or," it's "both-and." It is repentance *and* faith. And long before Paul spelled that out in the New Testament, Zechariah was teaching it to the former exiles in the land of Judah.

Blessings on you this day as you study Zechariah's visions and wrestle with that paradox.

Notes

Notes

3

GODLY
LEADERSHIP
Zechariah 6:9-15

Central Question

What is my attitude toward the leaders God provides?

Scripture

Zechariah 6:9-15 The word of the LORD came to me: 10 Collect silver and gold from the exiles—from Heldai, Tobijah, and Jedaiah—who have arrived from Babylon; and go the same day to the house of Josiah son of Zephaniah. 11 Take the silver and gold and make a crown, and set it on the head of the high priest Joshua son of Jehozadak; 12 say to him: Thus says the LORD of hosts: Here is a man whose name is Branch: for he shall branch out in his place, and he shall build the temple of the LORD. 13 It is he that shall build the temple of the LORD; he shall bear royal honor, and shall sit upon his throne and rule. There shall be a priest by his throne, with peaceful understanding between the two of them. 14 And the crown shall be in the care of Heldai, Tobijah, Jedaiah, and Josiah son of Zephaniah, as a memorial in the temple of the LORD. 15 Those who are far off shall come and help to build the temple of the LORD; and you shall know that the LORD of hosts has sent me to you. This will happen if you diligently obey the voice of the LORD your God.

Reflecting

The first church I served after graduating from seminary was managed by a strong group of longtime members. These members were powerful businessmen in our small community. They understood how to manage contracts, employees, and finances. They were continually elected to key committees in the church because of their success in the community, and they had become comfortable in their church leadership roles. I came on staff under a new pastor the church had recently called. He set about the task of providing leadership to the church as well.

It was soon apparent to everyone that all the leaders were not on the same page. The pastor wanted to change some things. The lay leaders felt no change was necessary. The lay leaders wanted to tell the pastor how to do his job. The pastor felt that was not necessary. Over time, I watched the lay leaders reject the pastor's spiritual leadership and act in a very "unchristian" fashion. I also watched the pastor reject the wise managerial advice of the lay leaders in an effort to satisfy his pride and prove his authority. As you can imagine, before long the church erupted in conflict. Some members left the church; others were wounded and disenchanted—including me.

Eventually, I moved on to other ministry positions, but this first experience left me with the troubling question of what it really means to lead and how we are to exercise leadership in the church. How is spiritual leadership intertwined with administrative leadership?

It seemed to me that the spiritual dimension often had important truths that affected how churches should organize and implement their ministries. On the other hand, the administrative dimension also brought important concepts that, when properly implemented, helped the church fulfill its mission.

> **What does godly leadership look like?**

Studying

After giving the prophet a series of eight visions, God instructs Zechariah about what he should do next. God tells him to gather silver and gold and make a crown with the precious metals. Heldai, Tobijah, and Jedaiah, from whom he was to get the gold and silver, were probably recent arrivals from Babylon who resided at the home of Josiah. They had most likely traveled a long way with their gifts. They probably intended them as an offering toward the rebuilding of the temple.

In verse 11, God instructs Zechariah to place the crown on the head of Joshua, the high priest. Due to the confusing passage that follows, however, some scholars believe that Zerubbabel the governor was the one to be crowned. Zerubbabel is referred to as the "Branch" in Zechariah 3:8, for he was a direct descendant of King David's royal line, though he "sprouted" in the foreign land of Babylon. He was a rightful heir to the throne of Judah.

Twice in this passage, "crowns" are mentioned in the plural in the Hebrew text (vv. 11, 14). But only Joshua is identified as the one who will wear a crown. Why, then, is Joshua the one who is crowned? Some argue that Joshua's name was substituted for Zerubbabel's in 6:11 at a later time after Zerubbabel did not live up to the messianic hopes the people had for him. However, there is no real evidence for this substitution. More likely, Zechariah could not boldly pronounce Zerubbabel as king in the current political situation. Zerubbabel was an appointed governor who answered to the Persian emperor. To proclaim him king would have been viewed as an act of rebellion, thereby bringing the swift hammer of Persia's wrath upon the Israelites. To place a crown on Joshua's head, however, would not have been threatening since he was merely Israel's religious leader and not of the royal Davidic line.

The crown given to Joshua was meant to be shared. It was for the Davidic leader who sat on the throne and for the priest who stood at his side. Together, they were to have a peaceful understanding between them. Together, they were to rule the land. In keeping with Zechariah's theme, the prophet called the nation to a renewed spiritual identity alongside its restored national identity. Both aspects of their identity were required, and both called for capable leadership. Competent leadership is needed in both the civil and religious spheres, and

The ultimate fate of Zerubbabel is unknown. After his mention in Zechariah, he seems to disappear from view, so we are left with the mystery of whether this joint leadership venture ever took place, and, if so, how well it worked.

those leaders must work together. Rivalry is not an option. The words translated "peaceful understanding" (6:13) do not refer simply to peaceful, harmonious consultation. Rather they refer to consultation that has peace as its object. The point is to work together for peace. Civil, polite conversation about issues would not be enough. The mission was to achieve peace together.

These words are true not only for the nation of Judah but also for our nation. Our political culture often encourages rivalry in place of cooperation. At times, leaders are more concerned with their political positioning than with what is truly best for the people. God calls for leaders to work side by side with cooperative spirits of understanding.

Some scholars see a messianic thread in this passage. That is, they interpret the shared leadership of king and priest as a sign of the coming Messiah who will fulfill both roles. This perspective views the crowning of Joshua as a symbolic act that predicts a future when Judah, and ultimately the world, will come under the divine rule of God's Anointed One. We know that king and priest to be

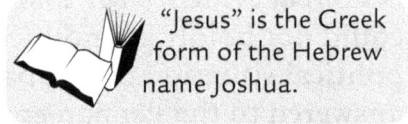
"Jesus" is the Greek form of the Hebrew name Joshua.

Jesus. He is the model for all leaders—one who served, showed compassion, demonstrated great patience, loved the poor, and attacked the hypocrisy of leaders who were more concerned with power and might than with following the leadership of God's Spirit.

Because the political circumstances didn't allow anyone to wear this symbolic crown, God instructed Zechariah to keep it in the temple as a memorial (6:14). There it would be an ongoing reminder of God's kingship and God's election of the Jewish nation. It would also be a memorial to Heldai, Tobijah, and Jedaiah, the Babylonian Jews who made an offering of the silver and gold from which it was made. When these men set out on the long journey from Babylon with their gifts for the

Joshua the High Priest, from *Promptuarii Iconum Insigniorum*, 1553

temple, they had no idea that their offering would have such profound meaning. It reminded the people that God remembered them and that a King was coming.

Was there any doubt among the people that Zechariah's words came from God? Were they uncertain about this joint venture between king and priest? That is a possibility, since God gives them the assurance of 6:15. Once they saw people coming from far off to rebuild the temple, they would know that what Zechariah had said was true. Zechariah looked forward to the day when more exiles would return to make the long-desired hope a reality.

Understanding

Judah needed leadership at this time of national reemergence. Someone needed to give direction to the rebuilding of the temple. Someone needed to manage disputes, oversee public policies, and ensure fair economic practices. God made it clear, however, that the nation also needed spiritual leadership. God intended for administrative and spiritual leaders to stand side by side. They were to share a peaceful understanding between them. Each leader had his proper role, but those roles were so intertwined that one could not be separated from the other.

I don't think Zechariah was saying that dual leadership is necessarily the answer for all nations or even for God-directed organizations such as the church. I do, however, think God was making the point that in God's kingdom, spiritual leadership is just as necessary as every other kind of leadership. We need women and men who can lead the church with gifts of administration and vision, but we also need strong spiritual leaders. Church leaders, whether lay or clergy, can and should make decisions that are grounded in prayer and the will of God. Similarly, national leaders can and should make decisions that flow through the spiritual dimension, that are in tune with God's desire for the nation.

How can we know what God desires for our nation? How can Christians seek answers to this question that do not merely impose our political preferences on God?

When leaders differ on what should be done and how to approach a problem, the first task is not to build barriers and fortify the different positions for battle. Rather, the solution must be found in respecting one another, in joining together in seeking the will of God, and in finding peaceful understanding together.

God seeks leaders who can combine both the administrative and spiritual dimensions. Such leaders understand the need for both dimensions to work together.

What About Me?

• *God calls leaders.* God called Zechariah to bring a prophetic message. God called Zerubbabel to lead the rebuilding of the temple. God called Joshua to give spiritual leadership to the nation. These leaders worked in concert to rebuild Judah in the years after the return from exile. God still calls leaders today. Each leader may have a different function, a different expertise, or a different set of skills, but God desires that all leaders work together for the common good.

• *We can all lead in small and large ways.* Those returning from Babylon—Heldai, Tobijah, and Jedaiah—played a vital role in this lesson's passage. They brought gifts that Zechariah used to make an important symbolic crown. This crown's placement in the temple was a memorial to their offering. Leaders come in all shapes and sizes. Many leaders never receive honor for their contributions like these men in our text did. Even so, each of us has gifts to offer. You are a leader if you organize the Sunday school class picnic or mentor a child. In sharing your spiritual insight during a Bible study class discussion, you give leadership. God's kingdom is made up of many leaders who seek to under- stand God's desires and fulfill them.

• *Choose leaders who take the spiritual dimension seriously.* In America we benefit from the strict separation of church and state. This does not, however, mean that Christians should never assess how sensitive our leaders are to the things of God. We want men and women leading our nation who take the time to listen for God's voice. Although it may seem obvious, we want the same thing for the leaders in our church. Unfortunately, this does not always hold true. Leading from a secular, political, or managerial focus alone is never sufficient. In the same way, leading from self-righteous spiritual pride is just as dangerous. God desires leaders who use the best administrative practices available. God also desires leaders who humbly seek the will of God in every decision.

Resources

Chad Brand and Charles Draper, eds., *Holman Illustrated Bible Dictionary* (Nashville: Holman, 2003).

Peter C. Craigie, *Twelve Prophets*, vol. 2 (Philadelphia: Westminster, 1985).

C. F. Keil and F. Delitzsch, *Commentary on the Old Testament*, vol. 10 (Grand Rapids: Eerdmans, 1982 [reprint]).

D. Winton Thomas and Theodore Cuyler Speers, "The Book of Zechariah," *The Interpreter's Bible*, vol. 6 (Nashville: Abingdon, 1956).

John D. W. Watts, "Zechariah," *The Broadman Bible Commentary*, vol. 7 (Nashville: Broadman, 1972).

GODLY
LEADERSHIP

Zechariah 6:9-15

Introduction

Picture two men talking to each other in 520 BC. They were both born in Babylon, but have recently immigrated to Judah. Life in Judah was new and strange to them. They had grown up in a foreign land, surrounded by foreign gods, and with little sense of what life used to be like in their ancestors' homeland. As the children of exiles, they had also grown up bitter, disillusioned, and suspicious of both religious and secular leaders.

"How goes it with you, my friend?" one asks the other.

"I'm managing," the other says, "but life here in Judah isn't much better than life in Babylon."

"I know what you mean. I can't find work, our family is on the brink of starvation, and it seems that all our leaders can think about is building a new temple."

"I hear you. We're all struggling to survive, but to hear Zerubbabel, Joshua, and Zechariah talk, you'd think building that temple was the most important thing in our lives."

"Frankly, I think those three are out of touch with reality. Judah can't afford a luxurious temple right now."

"True. But don't expect to hear anything different from them. They have their agenda, and they're going to stick to it."

"You know, I don't trust Governor Zerubbabel—or Joshua, the high priest, either. And I'm starting to think that Zechariah is in cahoots with both of them. I think they're all a little suspect."

That conversation, or something like it, was probably common in Judah when Zechariah wrote his prophecy. The people of Judah struggled to make ends meet. They didn't have much hope for the future and were suspicious of anyone in authority. One of the things Zechariah wanted to do was restore the people's trust in their leaders. Throughout his writings, he supports Zerubbabel and Joshua and presents them as agents of God. It was, without a doubt, a tough sell.

Our verses this lesson focus on a coronation. Zechariah tries to give those two imaginary Jews (and a host of others just like them) a new vision of what life could be like in Judah and a new respect for their God-given leaders.

The Coronation

Our focal passage can be divided into four sections:

• *Making the Crown* (6:9-11). The crown was to be made from gold and silver contributed by exiles who had recently returned from Babylon.

• *Crowning the "Branch"* (6:12-13). God declares, "Here is a man whose name is Branch: for he shall branch out in his place, and he shall build the temple of the LORD" (v. 12). Since the crown had just been placed on Joshua's head, it would seem this verse is referring to him, but verse 13 makes us think the "Branch" is actually Zerubbabel: "It is he that shall build the temple of the LORD; he shall bear royal honor, and shall sit upon his throne and rule." Joshua, the high priest, is to join him in this task: "There shall be a priest by his throne, with peaceful understanding between the two of them." Zerubbabel and Joshua were to work hand in hand to lead in the building of the temple.

• *Storing the Crown* (6:14). After the coronation, the crown was to be taken to the temple, where it would be a memorial. That crown would remind the people that God wanted the temple rebuilt and that God had ordained Joshua and Zerubbabel to lead in its construction.

• *Reinforcements from Afar* (6:15). This verse promises reinforcements from afar (probably more exiles arriving from Babylon) who would help with the building of the temple. If the task seemed overwhelming to the people of Judah, Zechariah offered the hope that help was on the way.

When you look at these verses as a whole, you see what Zechariah was trying to do: affirm Judah's leaders, get the people to remember the will of God, and motivate them to get on with the construction of the temple. In telling them of the crown and spelling out the specifics of the coronation, Zechariah was showing the people of Judah how good things could happen among them. He gave them a vision of how good life could be in Judah.

How Good Things Happen

If the people of Judah were to follow God's will and experience "the good life," Zechariah said, they would have to display the following characteristics:

First, *a shared vision*. They had to quit pulling against each other and start pulling in the same direction. Imagine how hectic and chaotic life must have been in those days. People were returning to Judah after years in Babylon. Many spoke a foreign language, spent foreign currency, ate foreign foods, and perhaps even worshiped foreign gods.

This ragtag, diverse bunch of people needed something or someone to bring them together. Zechariah had an inspired idea: let's bring them together around the worship of God, and let's make that happen by rebuilding the temple. The book of Zechariah is really about getting the people of Judah to share the same vision. Zechariah was trying to get the people on the same page by getting them to focus on the temple and, more importantly, the God of the temple.

Second, *competent leadership*. The people of Judah would thrive with good, godly people to lead them, and Zechariah believed Zerubbabel and Joshua fit the bill. They were the right men for the right time, in his eyes. He was going to support them. Finding and affirming competent leaders is always crucial business for a nation.

Third, *loyal followers*. People like our two fictional characters griping about their leaders were quite common in Zechariah's time. He probably heard their barbs and sarcastic remarks every day. But he knew that throwing stones at Zerubbabel and Joshua (and even at him!) was a futile activity. It might feel good to throw stones, but it doesn't accomplish anything productive. So,

Zechariah was a cheerleader for the governor and the high priest. He wanted others to become cheerleaders as well. Zechariah's message in a nutshell was, "Let's quit being critical followers and start being loyal followers, and we'll be amazed what we can accomplish together."

Fourth, *secular and spiritual leaders on the same page.* In Zechariah's vision of Judah's life, the secular and spiritual leaders work in harmony to accomplish good things. Zerubbabel, the governor, is pictured as working side by side with Joshua, the high priest. Politician and preacher joined hands for the good of the people.

Fifth, *a tent wide enough to include any who want to help.* Zechariah's vision for Judah involved reinforcements coming from afar to help shoulder the load. True, they wouldn't be perfect people. They would be desperate stragglers, wandering in from Babylon. But if they wanted to help—if they, too, could catch the vision of the new thing God wanted to do—they were welcome to come. This was to be a movement marked by the motto, "Whosoever will may come."

Sixth, *a good, godly heritage that was remembered and celebrated.* This whole scene of making the crown, having a coronation, and storing the crown in the temple was about creating memories. The people were to mark their memories with significant symbols and celebrations. Then they would be able to remember the day the people came home from exile, joined together in a noble endeavor, and rebuilt the temple of God.

By creating memory markers, the people could do what was commanded in Deuteronomy:

> Keep these words that I am commanding you today in your heart. Recite them to your children and talk about them when you are at home and when you are away, when you lie down and when you rise. Bind them as a sign on your hand, fix them as an emblem on your forehead, and write them on the doorposts of your house and on your gates. (Deut 6:6-9)

Zechariah's depiction of the coronation served as a vehicle to remind the people of Judah what they needed to do to live "the good life." If they had those six characteristics, they would be blessed as a nation.

Life in the Real World

When we read the components of Zechariah's vision for Judah, we may well have a Judah-like response: "In his dreams!" The world the prophet describes sounds wonderful, but life in the real world doesn't come close to matching Zechariah's depiction of it. In our own country, life is so diverse and multi-everything that we have no shared vision at all. Our leaders seem anything *but* competent. Grumbling and griping are favorite pastimes. Our secular and spiritual leaders seem to have completely different agendas. Prejudice and parochialism keep us from working together. And what memory markers we have of God's work among us have been forgotten by most of our citizens. For all of his good intentions, Zechariah may sound to us like a pious dreamer.

In reality, Judah wasn't exactly the perfect place Zechariah envisioned it to be, either. The people certainly didn't have a common dream. Zerubbabel and Joshua were not exceptional leaders, nor were they in complete harmony with one another. The people of Judah had a hard time welcoming newcomers to their land. And most of them had spiritual amnesia. They didn't have a clue about what God had done for them in the past. In other words, even in his own day, Zechariah was a pious dreamer!

But what is wrong with that? When things seem to be in shambles and discouragement reigns supreme, what is wrong with someone trying to remind us how good life can be? What is wrong with some pious dreamer coming along to help us remember how life is supposed to be lived? In a world where everything once nailed down is coming loose, what is so wrong with someone giving us a vision of how rich life can be if we re-nail a few key planks in place?

Conclusion

Certainly, when we take these verses and try to apply them to our personal lives, we can see some of the planks that need to be nailed back in place. Take Zechariah's pious dreaming, relate it to your life, and ponder the following questions.

Do I have a vision of what my life can be? What our nation can be?

Am I a competent, compassionate leader in my family? Office? Church?

Am I an encouraging follower of government, work, and church leaders? Or have I become negative and critical?

Can I support the best of my nation's goals? Can I embrace the heartbeat of my church's mission?

Do I include any person who wants to be in my life? Or have I erected unconscious walls that keep some people out?

Am I erecting symbols and having coronations that remind me of what God has done in my life? My family? My church? My nation?

Let's at least give Zechariah his due. He hadn't been swallowed by the negativism of his culture. It's all too easy to join the chorus of people down on life, down on government, down on church, and down on other people. It's all too easy to become a cynic and to think that throwing stones somehow makes us superior to those naïve idealists still working to make things better.

Before we write Zechariah off as just another dreamer out of touch with reality, let's acknowledge his strengths. He believed in the providence of God. He believed in the future of Judah. And he believed that he himself had a purpose in the eternal scheme of things.

"Pious dreamer?" Maybe so. But "inspiring role model" and "contagious leader" might be descriptions that fit Zechariah, too.

Notes

Notes

JUST
LIVING

Zechariah 7

Central Question

What can I do to help create a just society?

Scripture

Zechariah 7 In the fourth year of King Darius, the word of the LORD came to Zechariah on the fourth day of the ninth month, which is Chislev. 2 Now the people of Bethel had sent Sharezer and Regem-melech and their men, to entreat the favor of the LORD, 3 and to ask the priests of the house of the LORD of hosts and the prophets, "Should I mourn and practice abstinence in the fifth month, as I have done for so many years?" 4 Then the word of the LORD of hosts came to me: 5 Say to all the people of the land and the priests: When you fasted and lamented in the fifth month and in the seventh, for these seventy years, was it for me that you fasted? 6 And when you eat and when you drink, do you not eat and drink only for yourselves? 7 Were not these the words that the LORD proclaimed by the former prophets, when Jerusalem was inhabited and in prosperity, along with the towns around it, and when the Negeb and the Shephelah were inhabited? 8 The word of the LORD came to Zechariah, saying: 9 Thus says the LORD of hosts: Render true judgments, show kindness and mercy to one another; 10 do not oppress the widow, the orphan, the alien, or the poor; and do not devise evil in your hearts against one another. 11 But they refused to listen, and turned a stubborn shoulder, and stopped their ears in order not to hear. 12 They made their hearts adamant in order not to hear the law and the words that the LORD of hosts had sent by his spirit through the former prophets. Therefore great wrath came from the LORD of hosts. 13 Just as, when I called, they would not hear, so, when they called, I would not hear, says the LORD of hosts, 14 and I scattered them with a whirlwind among all the nations that they had not known. Thus the land they left was desolate, so that no one went to and fro, and a pleasant land was made desolate.

Reflecting

In early 2011, a major blizzard blew through most of the Midwest. In Oklahoma, where I live, meteorologists predicted fifty-miles-an-hour sustained winds, five-foot snowdrifts, and sub-zero temperatures. As the time approached, grocery stores were emptied of food, and there was a run on antifreeze, de-icer, and snow shovels at the hardware stores. The evening before the storm, my wife reminded me that I needed to check on the outside water spigots to make sure they wouldn't freeze. When I checked the one on the north side of my house, I discovered that someone had already put a small Styrofoam insulator over the spout. Wow! Someone, probably my neighbor, had seen that I was not prepared and had done a nice thing.

The storm came and went as predicted. On the third day after the storm, I was standing in my open garage looking out at the snow when my neighbor to the north crunched by in his overcoat and boots. "Hey," I called, "are you the one who put the insulator on my water spigot? Thanks. I really appreciate that. That was nice of you." He answered back, "Yeah, I did that, but in all honesty I wasn't thinking about you. I just didn't want your pipes to burst and flood my garage."

How often are the acts of our lives, however religious or self-less they appear, really for our own benefit? I thought it was significant, however, that my neighbor was honest about his motivations. Too often we do not have that kind of honesty even with ourselves. In this lesson, Zechariah addresses the issues of worship and kindness toward others. He calls us to look carefully at why we do what we do.

Studying

At the beginning of chapter 7, two years have passed since Zechariah's first visions. Much progress has been made on the temple reconstruction. When a question about worship arose among the people of Bethel, a town only a dozen miles to the north, they sent representatives to Jerusalem's priests and prophets to "entreat the favor of the LORD" regarding their question (7:2).

The men asked whether they should continue to mourn and fast in the fifth month of every year (7:3). This was not a trivial question. This particular fast commemorated the date in 586 BC when the Babylonians burned the temple and took the people into exile. But things had changed. The temple was well on its way to being rebuilt. Was there any need to continue their annual mourning? Shouldn't their sorrow be turned to joy and celebration?

Rather than give the delegation a straight answer immediately, Zechariah addressed the underlying purpose of the fasting and mourning period. He explored what this period meant for everyone, not merely those who asked the question (7:5-6). Zechariah asked if it was for God that they fasted. Fasting is an abstinence from food as a sign of a deep inner desire for help and repentance. Mourning rites indicated a sense of loss, not only of the temple, but also of God's presence and blessing in their lives. Was this really what was on the people's minds as they had fasted for the past seventy years? No. Zechariah argued that the yearly fasts and rituals were not about God but rather about the people. They had no real intention to repent or seek the renewed presence of God. Instead, the fasting and mourning had become expressions of self-pity and symbols of the desire to return to a time when things were good.

Whatever its original purpose, a ritual that loses its meaning is useless. God wanted transformed lives more than ritualistic worship. This is an important message for us to hear as well. When our forms and times of worship become more important than what they are intended to accomplish in bringing us closer to God, our worship is no different from the self-centered fasting and mourning of the returning exiles. Familiar hymns make us feel good. The style of worship makes us feel comfortable. Our private rituals of prayer and Bible reading give us a sense of completeness. But if they are only about what they give us, they miss the mark.

To punctuate his point, Zechariah reminds the people of the words of the prophets before the exile (7:7). Then the word of the Lord again comes to Zechariah to further remind the people of the message the prophets of old proclaimed (7:8-10). God does not want empty rituals. God wants a people who live justly. Justice has to do with rightly administering the covenant laws. Those laws included specific instructions like the Ten Commandments (Ex 20), but also included the more generalized laws of loving God (Deut 6:5) and loving neighbors (Lev 19:18). Justice refers not only to proper conduct within the law courts but also to how one should live in the community every day.

> He has told you, O mortal, what is good; and what does the Lord require of you but to do justice, and to love kindness, and to walk humbly with your God? (Mic 6:8)

In addition, God wants a people who demonstrate kindness and mercy to those around them, always showing compassion and caring. These are signs of a true relationship with God. The word translated "mercy" is the Hebrew word *chesed* and might also be translated "faithful love" (7:9). Mercy encompasses a broad spectrum of activity, including loyalty, steadfastness, and faithfulness as well as love. The word translated "kindness" ("compassion" in some translations) is related to the Hebrew word for womb and focuses primarily on a tender, maternal type of love (7:9).

In more specific terms, God called on the people to do what is right and just for the widows, orphans, aliens, and the poor (7:10). They should tend to the needs of the oppressed, the marginalized, the defenseless, the disadvantaged, and the helpless. God's people should be their advocates when they are mistreated and their voice when others who are less caring silence them. It is easy for us to become self-centered not only in our worship but also in our living.

Finally, Zechariah reminded the people what happened to their ancestors when they refused to listen to the message of the Lord through the prophets of the past (7:11-14). God's great wrath came upon them, the temple was destroyed, and they were sent into exile. When they turned to God in the midst of disaster, God chose not to hear them because they had not listened to God. This is a clear warning to the returning exiles—and to us.

Understanding

For almost seventy years, the Jewish people had spent every fifth month fasting and mourning their situation. In the beginning, it was because they were sorry for their sins. The message of the prophets had proven to be true. They had turned away from God, worshiped idols, and mistreated the poor and widows of the land. As a result, God stopped listening to them, and the Babylonian army destroyed all that was holy to them and took them from their promised land.

Over time, however, the Israelites forgot the real purpose of the yearly rituals of grief and mourning. Instead of sorrow and repentance for their sins, these rituals came to represent sorrow that life was difficult for them. They turned from God-centered worship to self-centered worship. They were in danger of repeating history by following in the steps of their ancestors.

Zechariah's message to them is a clear message to us as well. True worship—worship that humbly bends our knees before God and seeks God's will for our lives—is imperative. Worship, however, is much more than just showing up for a service on Sunday morning, singing a few hymns, and listening to a sermon. Worship is what we do with our lives every day. The rituals are nothing without justice, kindness, and mercy toward those who are marginalized in our world. Zechariah called the Jewish

> I appeal to you therefore, brothers and sisters, by the mercies of God, to present your bodies as a living sacrifice, holy and acceptable to God, which is your spiritual worship. Do not be conformed to this world, but be transformed by the renewing of your minds, so that you may discern what is the will of God—what is good and acceptable and perfect. (Rom 12:1-2)

nation, and us, to transformed lives that look beyond selfish desires and care deeply for the plight of others.

What About Me?

• *Are worship rituals good?* Although Zechariah chastised the people for their empty worship, he was not saying rituals as such are bad. Rather, they become worthless when they are performed in the wrong spirit or for the wrong reasons. Worship of all kinds is good and pleasing to God when we come to God honestly, humbly, and with a desire to hear and do God's will.

• *Is my worship self-serving?* We all have to stop and ask ourselves regularly, "Do I worship, pray, or participate in church activities because of what I get out of it?" If we are honest, many of us, especially those who have attended church for many years, find great personal satisfaction in regular worship. It gives us comfort and sometimes a nostalgic sense of peace. When these are the reasons we worship, though, we have lost our way.

• *What should justice, kindness, and mercy look like in my life?* The Bible speaks a great deal about these things. They were at the core of Zechariah's message. Put simply, they are the outward manifestation of our relationship with God. God has demonstrated justice, kindness, and mercy to each of us. God forgives us when we don't deserve it. God provides for us when we have nothing. God expects each of us to do the same for others in our world.

• *Who are the marginalized people around me for whom God wants me to care?* The Bible speaks of widows, orphans, aliens, and the poor. These were the ones with the fewest rights and advantages in Zechariah's day. Who are these people today in your community? Does this group include the vast number of people living below the poverty level, the mentally ill, the illegal aliens, the felons, or the homeless? These are the ones who most need to experience God's love through our demonstrations of justice, mercy, and kindness.

Resources

Kenneth L. Barker, "Zechariah," *The Expositor's Bible Commentary*, vol. 7, ed. Frank E. Gaebelein (Grand Rapids: Zondervan, 1985).

Chad Brand and Charles Draper, eds., *Holman Illustrated Bible Dictionary* (Nashville: Holman, 2003).

Peter C. Craigie, *Twelve Prophets*, vol. 2 (Philadelphia: Westminster, 1985).

D. Winton Thomas and Theodore Cuyler Speers, "The Book of Zechariah," *The Interpreter's Bible*, vol. 6 (Nashville: Abingdon, 1956).

John D. W. Watts, "Zechariah," *The Broadman Bible Commentary*, vol. 7 (Nashville: Broadman, 1972).

JUST
LIVING
Zechariah 7

Introduction

The first thing I do when I wake up in the morning is reach for my glasses on the table beside my bed. Without that simple act, I would be lost for the rest of the day. I would wander around half blind, stumbling and bumbling my way through life. Without my glasses, I couldn't pour my coffee, read the paper, recognize my wife, or drive to the grocery store. It is not overstating the case to say that without my glasses I would be a helpless invalid. That simple, unconscious act of reaching for my glasses is probably the most important thing I do all day.

Our verses from Zechariah this lesson are an invitation to put on our "spiritual glasses" so that we can see ourselves and our world more clearly. In Ephesians 1, the Apostle Paul prays that the Ephesians will have the eyes of their heart enlightened, and that is what these verses seek to do. Zechariah wanted his readers to have the eyes of their heart enlightened. He wanted them to look, in particular, in three directions: at their rituals, their relationships, and at people who are hurting.

If the people of Judah wanted to do more than stumble and bumble through life, they needed to have the eyes of their heart enlightened to see these three things clearly. We read Zechariah's words this lesson knowing that the same truth applies to us.

Looking at Our Rituals

Sometime around 518 BC, while the temple was still being built, a contingent from Bethel (in the former territory of the northern kingdom of Israel) came to Jerusalem with a question. They wanted to know if they were now free to discontinue a fast they had been observing for years. It was the fast of the fifth month, a fast that commemorated the burning of the temple in 587 BC. In essence, these visitors from Bethel were asking, "Now that the temple is being rebuilt, isn't it appropriate to give up the fast that commemorates its destruction?"

For many years, these people had observed a meaningful ritual. During the fifth month of every year, they fasted to mourn the loss of the temple in Jerusalem. But, with the building of the new temple, the reason for the fast was about to be eradicated. The ritual was about to lose its meaning. Would it be acceptable to give it up?

Zechariah's response speaks not only to those visitors from Bethel but to all of us who observe our rituals. In effect, he said, "A ritual can lose its meaning, and when it does, it is not only acceptable, but advisable, to let it go." Zechariah's response reminds us that rituals are good only as long as they jog our memory and nurture a rhythm and order in our lives. That's what rituals are supposed to do. They remind us of significant events, and they nurture our lives by giving us a regular and dependable rhythm. If there is no remembering or nurturing going on, it's time for the ritual to go.

No doubt, all of us have rituals that give meaning to our lives. We have personal rituals, family rituals, societal rituals, and church rituals. If we stop a moment and think about them, we will realize just how many rituals we *do* have. Our lives would be impoverished without our morning coffee and newspaper, the family meal together every Sunday, or the annual Christmas Eve service at church. Those events, and a hundred more rituals we have built into our lives, order our days and remind us of significant things. But rituals can outlive their purpose, and when they do, as with the fasting in Bethel, it's time for them to go.

For years, our family had a wonderful ritual. Every Christmas Eve, our family of four went to our church's candlelight service together, followed by a meal at our favorite restaurant. Then we all got up on Christmas morning, had breakfast, and opened our presents around the tree. It was perfect and enjoyable, and it gave our family both order and wonder. Sherry, our children, Stacy and Randel, and I enjoyed Christmas together the same way every year. Why would anyone want to change a tradition like that?

But circumstances changed. Stacy and Randel both got married and moved to Austin. Then they got family dogs. Then they had children. Coming to our house to continue the ritual became a chore. They had to load up children, dogs, and presents. The effort seemed tantamount to moving to a new house! The old ritual of our perfect and wonderful Christmas together as a family had become an ordeal for our children. They were coming for our benefit, but the magic and meaning of the ritual were gone.

So, we dropped it. This past Christmas, Sherry and I went to them. We don't have babies and dogs to haul around, so we just hopped in our car, drove to Austin, and celebrated Christmas there. It seemed a bit strange, but I'm sure our son and daughter were relieved not to have to make the arduous journey to be with Mom and Dad. Our old family ritual served us well for a long time, but it has now been officially retired.

Zechariah counseled the people from Bethel that the old fast in the fifth month had lost its meaning. It could justifiably be retired. Not only did the prophet give the people permission to drop it, he encouraged them to drop it. Rituals are important only as long as they are connected to meaning and wonder.

Looking at Our Relationships

Zechariah also invited the people of Judah to put on their spiritual glasses so they could clearly see their relationships with one another. He mentions three specific qualities to look for:

The first quality is *honesty*. The people were to "render true judgments" (7:9). That conjures up a courtroom setting where truth is spoken and justice is served. In their relationships with one another, they were not to be deceptive and duplicitous; they were to be scrupulously honest.

Most of us do not make a giant leap from honesty to dishonesty. It happens slowly, one "white lie" at a time. We gradually shade the truth a little, exaggerate ever so slightly, or practice miniscule deceptions. It all seems so harmless, but those little deceptions have a way of growing into big deceptions. Before we know it, we find ourselves mired in some kind of major lie. The only way to stay off the slippery slope of dishonesty is to render true judgments every day. Every day, we tell—and live—the truth. Every day, we fight off the temptation to render false judgments in our relationships.

The second quality is *kindness*. Zechariah encouraged the people of Judah to show kindness to one another. True kindness is a rare trait because it demands so much of us. Anyone who is kind has to have at least three characteristics: they must have good eyes that see the needs in another person's life, a good heart that is moved to compassion, and good hands that do something tangible to meet that person's needs.

Kindness can break down at any one of those three points. What if we don't have good eyes and are oblivious to the needs of the people around us? What if we don't have a good heart and aren't moved with compassion? And what if we see and feel but don't act? What if we don't have good hands that do tangible acts of love?

Let us simply admit that kindness is easier said than done, easier preached than lived. But nothing nurtures a relationship like simple acts of kindness.

The third quality is *mercy*. Zechariah encouraged the people of Judah to show mercy to each other. Mercy is even harder than kindness. Mercy is about forgiveness and grace. It's about staying in relationship with people who keep messing up, keep falling short of our expectations, and keep disappointing us. Mercy is God-like; it is the capacity to extend to the people in our lives the gracious spirit that God has extended to us in Christ. And, like kindness, mercy is easier to preach than to live.

As a pastor for many years, it was my great pleasure to perform the marriage ceremonies of many couples. I typically met with each couple for premarital counseling and did my best to get them off to a good start.

As I think about it now, though, I think Zechariah's counsel about relationships would have served me well in my premarital counseling. I think his three relational virtues are crucial to a good marriage; crucial, in fact, to any relationship. I could have said to those couples:

• Will you promise to be honest with each other? Will you work every day at rendering true judgments to one another?
• Will you promise to be kind to one another? Will you be attentive to one another, feel compassion for one another, and do little things to serve one another?
• Will you show mercy to one another? Will you forgive each other, knowing that each of you is flawed and imperfect? Will you make grace the foundation of your marriage?

I didn't use the book of Zechariah as a premarital counseling guide, but I could have. His counsel to build relationships that are marked by honesty, kindness, and mercy can help any couple start their marriage on the right foot.

Looking at "the Least of These"

Long before Jesus told his followers to take care of "the least of these" in his parable of the sheep and goats (Mt 25:31-46), Zechariah told the people of Judah to put on their spiritual glasses and see the hurting people around them: "Do not oppress the widow, the orphan, the alien, or the poor; and do not devise evil in your hearts against one another" (Zech 7:10).

But would any of us want to harm widows, orphans, aliens, or poor people? Are any of us who are "good, church-going people" capable of devising evil against "the least of these"? Probably not. But what we are capable of is ignoring them. We don't take care of them simply because they're not on our radar screen. Most of us don't live among widows, orphans, aliens, or poor people, so we just don't see them. Our neglect of them is the result of blindness, not meanness. It is a practical fact of ministry that we can't help people we don't see.

So, Zechariah called the people of Judah to open their eyes. "The least of these" were all around them. When we think about it, we realize they're all around us, too, if only we'll have the eyes of our heart enlightened enough to see them.

Conclusion

As I said, putting on my glasses every morning is probably my most important act of the day. Without that simple act, I'm doomed to a day of frustration and futility.

Zechariah knew that Judah was destined for frustration and futility, too, unless the people put on their spiritual glasses to see their rituals, their relationships, and the "least of these" in their society. If they saw those three things clearly, they could live justly and be godly people.

And what if they didn't do those three things? Well, Zechariah said they would suffer the same fate as their ancestors. Their ancestors had been given the same commands from God, but "they made their hearts adamant in order not to hear the law and the words that the Lord of hosts had sent by his spirit through the former prophets" (v. 12).

Their ancestors experienced the wrath of God and were scattered like a whirlwind among the nations. The final verse in chapter 7 is ominous: "Thus the land they left was desolate, so that no one went to and fro, and a pleasant land was made desolate" (v. 14).

God had placed before their ancestors an open door, but they refused to enter it. God had wanted them to get rid of empty ritual, foster good relationships, and take care of "the least of these." Their refusal to do those things led to their demise.

Zechariah was trying to make sure that history didn't repeat itself.

Notes

Notes

5

PROMISED
RESTORATION

Zechariah 8

Central Question

What aspects of my life need to experience God's restoring power?

Scripture

Zechariah 8 The word of the LORD of hosts came to me, saying:
2 Thus says the LORD of hosts: I am jealous for Zion with great
jealousy, and I am jealous for her with great wrath. 3 Thus says
the LORD: I will return to Zion, and will dwell in the midst of
Jerusalem; Jerusalem shall be called the faithful city, and the
mountain of the LORD of hosts shall be called the holy mountain.
4 Thus says the LORD of hosts: Old men and old women shall
again sit in the streets of Jerusalem, each with staff in hand
because of their great age. 5 And the streets of the city shall be
full of boys and girls playing in its streets. 6 Thus says the LORD
of hosts: Even though it seems impossible to the remnant of this
people in these days, should it also seem impossible to me, says
the LORD of hosts? 7 Thus says the LORD of hosts: I will save my
people from the east country and from the west country; 8 and I
will bring them to live in Jerusalem. They shall be my people
and I will be their God, in faithfulness and in righteousness.
9 Thus says the LORD of hosts: Let your hands be strong—you
that have recently been hearing these words from the mouths
of the prophets who were present when the foundation was laid
for the rebuilding of the temple, the house of the LORD of hosts.
10 For before those days there were no wages for people or for
animals, nor was there any safety from the foe for those who went

out or came in, and I set them all against one other. 11 But now I will not deal with the remnant of this people as in the former days, says the LORD of hosts. 12 For there shall be a sowing of peace; the vine shall yield its fruit, the ground shall give its produce, and the skies shall give their dew; and I will cause the remnant of this people to possess all these things. 13 Just as you have been a cursing among the nations, O house of Judah and house of Israel, so I will save you and you shall be a blessing. Do not be afraid, but let your hands be strong. 14 For thus says the LORD of hosts: Just as I purposed to bring disaster upon you, when your ancestors provoked me to wrath, and I did not relent, says the LORD of hosts, 15 so again I have purposed in these days to do good to Jerusalem and to the house of Judah; do not be afraid. 16 These are the things that you shall do: Speak the truth to one another, render in your gates judgments that are true and make for peace, 17 do not devise evil in your hearts against one another, and love no false oath; for all these are things that I hate, says the LORD. 18 The word of the LORD of hosts came to me, saying: 19 Thus says the LORD of hosts: The fast of the fourth month, and the fast of the fifth, and the fast of the seventh, and the fast of the tenth, shall be seasons of joy and gladness, and cheerful festivals for the house of Judah: therefore love truth and peace. 20 Thus says the LORD of hosts: Peoples shall yet come, the inhabitants of many cities; 21 the inhabitants of one city shall go to another, saying, "Come, let us go to entreat the favor of the LORD, and to seek the LORD of hosts; I myself am going." 22 Many peoples and strong nations shall come to seek the LORD of hosts in Jerusalem, and to entreat the favor of the LORD. 23 Thus says the LORD of hosts: In those days ten men from nations of every language shall take hold of a Jew, grasping his garment and saying, "Let us go with you, for we have heard that God is with you."

Reflecting

My older brother enjoys woodworking. It is a gift that requires a great deal of precision, patience, and knowledge—not to mention expensive tools. My brother is also a scavenger. I mean that in the kindest way. A few years ago, he came upon a large piece of furniture in the middle of the road. At first he couldn't tell what it was because it was so broken. Pieces were scattered everywhere. Evidently it had fallen off someone's truck, hit the hard asphalt surface, and shattered into many pieces. No doubt the sad and upset owners saw it as a total loss and decided to abandon it. Being the scavenger he is, however, my brother saw it as a gold mine. Despite my sister-in-law's objection, he stopped his van and scurried back and forth across the road to collect all the pieces.

Eventually, he reassembled his find like a jigsaw puzzle, glued the split pieces, rehinged the doors, fixed the broken drawers, sanded the scarred wood, and refinished the piece to a point that even a close observer couldn't tell it was once abandoned as worthless. He still displays this beautifully restored antique oak armoire in his home as one of his masterpieces.

When the Babylonians destroyed Jerusalem and took the broken people into captivity, the Jews wondered if restoration with God would ever be possible. From their abandoned place, they fasted and mourned, praying for restoration. God heard their cry, rebuilt their temple, and restored their lives to newness once again.

Studying

Because of Judah's irreverence toward God before the exile, God's jealousy for Zion was great. Eventually, after much patience, God chose to abandon Jerusalem, proclaiming, "the faithful city has become a whore!" (Isa 1:21). Now, however, through Zechariah God proclaimed good news. God's long-awaited restoration had arrived. God would return to Zion and dwell there. Jerusalem would once again be called the "faithful city" (Zech 8:3).

God not only promised restoration for Jerusalem but also provided beautiful word pictures of what it would look like. Can you see the old men and women sitting in the narrow streets propped on their canes watching the children laugh and play (8:4-5)? This is a wonderfully serene picture of multiple generations sharing life together with the innocent exuberance of children and the quiet wisdom of the aged.

Perhaps it was a vision they could not even fathom. But what they perceived to be impossible was possible with God (8:6). Even when the wondrous possibility of restoration seems beyond our comprehension, we can be assured it is never beyond God's power. God pointed them to a new future in which the past was forgotten and scattered people would be reunited. God would once again be their God, and they would be God's people (8:7-8).

After painting this wonderful picture of restoration, God encourages them to continue to rebuild the temple. "Let your hands be strong" (8:9), don't give up, and "Do not be afraid" (8:13). It is true that even a few years before, when the prophets encouraged them to lay the foundation, things were rough (8:9). There hadn't been enough money, safety, or peace to make much progress (8:10). Now, however, God is ready to announce that things will be different (8:11). Peace will prevail, the vines will produce, and the skies will offer the necessary moisture (8:12). They didn't need to worry any longer about shortage of money or lack of safety. "I will save you," God says (8:13). Other nations would no longer curse them. Quite the contrary, they would now be a blessing to other nations. God alludes here to the original covenant with Abram in which God promised that Abram's descendants would be a blessing (Gen 12:2). When we have a restored covenant relationship with God, we become God's instruments of blessing to the world once again.

Restoration with God requires confession and acknowledgment of our sins. This was something the Jews had been doing for seventy years. But sorrowful words are never enough. What God truly wants is repentance. In verses 16-17, God reminds them of what their covenant relationship is all about. God says, "These are the things that you shall do" (8:16). The things God mentions address problems the people had in the past and were already starting to demonstrate again. They are things that still give us trouble in our lives: lying rather than speaking the truth, taking advantage of people rather than treating them

The gates of cities in ancient Palestine often had built-in stone benches where people could sit with friends, transact business, make legal contracts, make public proclamations, and hold "court."

justly, and devising evil for others in our hearts rather than good (8:17). The list God gave them made it evident that a restored relationship with God is closely connected to our relationship with other people. How can we be right with God when we continue to mistreat those around us?

In Zechariah 7:3, a delegation came to Jerusalem to ask the priests and prophets if they should continue the fasts and mourning rituals that had begun seventy years earlier when Jerusalem fell. Now the prophet finally provides the answer they sought: fasting and mourning are no longer necessary. There will now be seasons of joy and gladness (8:19). No longer do they need to be sad and penitent for their sins. God has put their sins behind them and offers them a new beginning. That is what it means to be restored. As a result, sorrow turns to joy.

> God is referred to as "Lord of hosts" more than forty times in Zechariah 1–8. God is indeed the Lord of hosts, and some day everyone will know it.

Just as the men from Bethel traveled to Jerusalem to seek the favor of the Lord, in the future people from all over the world, Jew and Gentile alike, will come to Jerusalem to seek God's favor (8:21-22). There will be no doubt that God is with the people of Judah. When Gentiles see a Jewish person traveling toward Jerusalem, they will grab hold of his garment and say, "Let us go with you" (8:23). God is with all those who come to him. God dwells in us, guides us, and offers restoration to us through the constant divine presence.

Understanding

It is a terrifying thing to stand in the presence of God when we have sinned. The people of Judah experienced this during the exile. Thankfully, however, through God's grace, restoration is possible. When we return to God, our sins are put behind us, and God's wrath turns to blessing. When we come to God with penitent hearts, we have no need to fear. God will turn our sorrow into great celebration!

God's willingness to forgive us and restore us into an intimate relationship is often beyond our grasp to comprehend. Perhaps we can understand intellectually the suffering of Jesus on the cross for our sins, the need for his sacrifice to bring forgiveness, and the hope of new life that resurrection provides. Emotionally, however, many of us have difficulty allowing these truths to free us from our sense of guilt and sorrow. We continue to want to figuratively fast and mourn our past failures.

We don't have to keep beating ourselves up. The fasting and mourning are no longer necessary. A new hopeful future is before us if we are prepared to turn aside from sin and give our lives to God once more. John tells us, "If we confess our sins, he who is faithful and just will forgive us our sins and cleanse us from all unrighteousness" (1 Jn 1:9). Zechariah reminds us that nothing is impossible with God, not even the restoration of relationships that once seemed beyond repair. No wonder God calls us to joy, gladness, and cheerful festivals.

What About Me?

• *Your relationship with God can be restored.* I occasionally talk to people, even Christians, who tell me that their lives have strayed so far from God that rebuilding that relationship is no longer possible. I try to remind them that the limitations they feel are from their side only. God can do all things, including forgiving the worst of sinners. Are we willing to accept that forgiveness and seek God again?

• *God desires restoration with everyone.* God continuously pursues a relationship with each of us. Certainly there are times when God may discipline us or allow our sinful lives to carry us to whatever sorrowful depths we cause. Nevertheless, God does not abandon us. Rather, he keeps returning to us for continual opportunities for intimacy.

• *Restoration is made possible through Jesus Christ.* For centuries, the people of God struggled with how to "get right" with God. They sacrificed animals, observed months of fasting, and made up new rules to make sure they didn't offend God. Eventually, God traded all these measures for the sacrifice of Jesus. God sent Jesus, his only Son, into the world to die on the cross for our sins. His death became a substitute for our own. When we believe in him and what he did for us, our sins are forgiven and a relationship with God begins.

• *Restoration is a two-way street.* God's covenant with Abram was one of promise. God said, "I will be your God and bless you." However, God also required that Abram and his descendants be God's people. God requires that we be obedient, live righteously, and show justice. Regardless of how much God pursues us, if we are not willing to turn from sin and live differently, that relationship will always be strained.

• *Restoration should be celebrated.* I may not be a dancer or a singer, but I can certainly experience the overwhelming joy of complete forgiveness and newly restored relationship with the Creator of the world. Sin in our lives is tragic. Forgiveness requires celebration!

Resource

Kenneth L. Barker, "Zechariah," *The Expositor's Bible Commentary*, vol. 7, ed. Frank E. Gaebelein (Grand Rapids: Zondervan, 1985).

Peter C. Craigie, *Twelve Prophets*, vol. 2 (Philadelphia: Westminster, 1985).

D. Winton Thomas and Theodore Cuyler Speers, "The Book of Zechariah," *The Interpreter's Bible*, vol. 6 (Nashville: Abingdon, 1956).

John D. W. Watts, "Zechariah," *The Broadman Bible Commentary*, vol. 7 (Nashville: Broadman, 1972).

PROMISED RESTORATION

Zecharaiah 8

Introduction

Humpty-Dumpty is more than a familiar nursery rhyme; it is also the storyline in many a person's life. Some people, moving comfortably through life, suddenly have a great fall. Something happens—a death, divorce, job loss, sickness, accident, or some other unforeseen calamity—and their lives are irrevocably broken. They become defined by that tragic event, and nothing can put them back together again. Their serenity, their happiness, and their confidence are shattered forever.

We have all known people like this, Humpty-Dumpty people who have such a great fall they can't seem to recover from it. Whenever we see that, it sobers and shakes us and reminds us that bad things do happen to good people.

But we also know people who somehow recover from a tragic fall. They survive the calamity and come out on the other side battered and bruised, but alive and well, and maybe even stronger than before. These people remind us that the Humpty-Dumpty rhyme is not an inevitable storyline for everyone. Sometimes Humpty-Dumpty does get put back together again. Whenever it happens, we take heart. If that person can survive such a fall, we think to ourselves, maybe we can, too.

Our passage this lesson from Zechariah is addressed to Humpty-Dumpty people. The people who had come back to Judah after being in Babylon for years were discouraged and depressed. They had had a great fall, and they wondered, no doubt, if anything or anyone could put them back together again. Zechariah wrote to assure them that God was more than capable of restoring their lives—as individuals and as a nation.

Zechariah 8 is a ringing endorsement of the power of God to put Humpty-Dumpty back together again.

Ten Promises to Judah

Sort through the entire chapter, and you will discover ten promises Zechariah gave the people of Judah:

(1) *God's relentless devotion to Judah* (8:1-2). God is "jealous" for the people of Judah and will express wrath toward those who oppress them.
(2) *God dwelling in Jerusalem with the people of Judah* (8:3). God pledges to "dwell in the midst of Jerusalem" among the people and to stay with them.
(3) *Young and old will mingle in the streets of Jerusalem* (8:4-5). When God resides in Jerusalem, it will be a place for children to play and old people to feel safe.
(4) *God can accomplish the impossible* (8:6). God can do what looks impossible to the people of Judah.
(5) *More exiles will arrive and God will bless them* (8:7-8). More people will return to Judah, and God will renew his covenant with them.
(6) *The completion of the temple and the restoration of Judah's dignity and prosperity* (8:9-13). These verses begin and end with the admonition to "let your hands be strong" because God is going to do great things among the people.
(7) *Certain blessing to obedient people* (8:14-17). If the people will speak the truth, render judgments of honesty and peace, not devise evil against one another, and love no false oath, they can be certain of God's blessing.
(8) *Fasts becoming feasts* (8:18-19). All of the fasts the people have been observing will be turned into "seasons of joy and gladness."
(9) *A pilgrimage of foreigners to Jerusalem* (8:20-22). Life in Judah will be so blessed that people from other nations will want to experience it.
(10) *Foreigners will want to know Judah's God* (8:23). People from other lands will want to know the God who has so blessed Judah.

The purpose of the entire chapter is to assure those Humpty-Dumpty Jews that God was still with them and that God would put their lives back together again. The ten promises of Zechariah 8 all really say the same thing: "God is still working in and among you to bless your life."

A God of Open Doors

As I studied Zechariah 8, I thought of people I know who have "had a great fall." I have known many people who have had to walk through the valley of the shadow of death, disease, divorce, or defeat. Some have been almost destroyed by their tragedy and, at least to this point, haven't recovered from it.

But I think, too, of friends who have gone through some terrible "exile experience" but have emerged triumphant on the other side. They have survived their tragedy, rebuilt their lives, and renewed their faith in God. I sometimes wonder if I would have had the faith to endure what they have had to endure.

I think, for example, of my friend Tony. Tony got married, had a couple of kids, and became a pastor. But then he had a great fall. No, actually, he had several great falls. He went through a painful divorce. He then opened a counseling center that failed and left him bankrupt. He became a pastor again but left that church hurt and wounded. One of his children fell into a life of drugs and alcohol and died an early death. How much should one person have to take? My friend Tony has been through it.

But here's the amazing thing about him. He is one of the most upbeat people I know. Passing through all of that fire didn't burn him; it refined him. He married a woman who has been through some fires herself, and he now has a great marriage, teaches at a local college, is active in his church, and stands as living proof that Humpty-Dumpty can be put back together again. Tony's middle name is Resilient.

That kind of story reminds us that God is a God of open doors. That's one of the main lessons we can learn from our study of Zechariah. God never gave up on Judah and kept opening doors for them. And God never gives up on us, either. God keeps opening doors for us, too. If I had to sum up the message of Zechariah in one sentence, it would be that God is in the business of putting Humpty-Dumpty back together again.

As you study Zechariah 8 this lesson, you will have an opportunity to offer that good news to the Humpty-Dumpty people in your class—which is probably all of them!

The Ingredients of Personal Renewal

What would Zechariah say are the ingredients of personal renewal? As we have moved through the first eight chapters of his book, several of those ingredients have become clear. Zechariah's plan for both national and personal renewal would include at least the following four ingredients:

First, *know that God is good*. Zechariah's God is demanding and righteous, but also full of love and grace. Zechariah's God is relentless in pursuit of Judah, even though the people have done nothing to deserve God's favor.

The first ingredient in any plan for renewal is the conviction that God is *for* us. If we ever doubt that, all we have to do is reread Paul's celebration of God's love in Romans 8. If God is for us, he exults, who—or what—can possibly be against us? Once we know that God loves us and is for us, we're on the way to personal renewal.

Second, know that *God is active in your life*. Not only is God for us, God is moving, acting, and making things happen. Zechariah pictures God as moving among the people, pitching his tent among them, drawing people to Jerusalem, and renewing the covenant with them. In short, Zechariah's God is not a relic of the past or a doddering Old Man Upstairs; his God is dynamic and working—not only in Judah's history but also in the lives of individuals.

That's the second ingredient in an effective plan for renewal. We know that God is not only for us but that God is actively working in our lives to bless us. As the Apostle Paul put it to the Philippians, "I am confident of this, that the one who began a good work among you will bring it to completion by the day of Jesus Christ" (Phil 1:6). The God who created us and redeemed us through Christ will keep working in our lives to bring us to completion. We are each a work in progress, and God is intimately involved in the process.

Third, *know that repentance is crucial.* Zechariah kept calling the people of Judah to repent and reminding them that God has certain standards that make life worth living. When we fall short of those standards, we're dooming ourselves to a life of failure and disappointment.

As we have seen, repentance is not a negative thing at all. Repentance is realizing we're on the road to failure and disappointment and deciding to get on a different road that leads to success and joy. Some roads lead to death, and some roads lead to life, and God has given us the freedom to decide which road we will take. Repentance is the liberating decision to choose the road that will take us to life.

Fourth, *know the lessons of history.* Zechariah kept reminding the people of Judah of their past, how their ancestors had taken the wrong road, and how they themselves had, at times, taken the wrong road and suffered for it. As we have seen, one of the messages in the book of Zechariah is the old adage that those who don't learn the lessons of history are destined to repeat them.

If we want to experience personal renewal, knowing the lessons of history is crucial. We learn from the experience of others, and we also look back at our own experiences and learn from them, too. If we learn the lessons of history, we are rescued from a life of insanity in which we do the same things over and over again and somehow expecting different results. We take stock, make some new commitments, get on a new road, and start experiencing personal renewal.

Get to the core of Zechariah's message to Judah, and that's what you see. If the people were going to experience national and personal renewal, they would need a good God, they would need an active God, they would need to keep repenting, and they would have to learn the lessons of history. That plan was sound in the sixth century BC, and it still rings true today.

Conclusion

At the age of thirty-five, Philip Simmons was diagnosed with ALS (Lou Gehrig's Disease) and was immediately confronted with his own mortality. It was the kind of experience we would all just as soon avoid. Being diagnosed with a terminal illness at the age of thirty-five is about as bad as it gets.

Philip Simmons resigned his position as a professor of English, retreated to a cabin in the woods, and penned a fine book about his struggle. In the book, he is not pious or sentimental but completely candid and straightforward about his feelings. He writes truthfully of his fears and hopes, and when you read his book, you feel you are in the presence of an honest man. The title of the book is telling: *Learning to Fall: The Blessings of an Imperfect Life* (New York: Bantam, 2002).

When we study a book like Zechariah, we are at first put off by the book's bizarre visions and seeming remoteness from the modern world. Frankly, most of us, when given the opportunity to study Zechariah, would just as soon not. We think of it as weird, dated, and boring.

But once we understand the occasion that prompted the book and Zechariah's purpose in writing it, we can overlook some of its eccentricities. The book of Zechariah was addressed to people who were trying to build a life of hope in a most discouraging situation, and its purpose was to offer hope and renewal to those people.

For all of his strangeness, Zechariah was simply trying to teach those Humpty-Dumpty people how to fall, how to rise up from their tragedy, and how to experience the blessings of their imperfect lives.

Notes

Notes

nextsunday
STUDIES

1 Peter
Keep Hope Alive

This study of First Peter focuses on keeping hope alive in the face of pressures and circumstances that could possibly extinguish it completely, or worse, turn authentic faith into a pale replica of the real thing.

Advent Virtues

The phrase "holiday rush" is not an exaggeration. The frantic pace required to purchase gifts, bake holiday foods, and attend Christmas parties, plays, and performances takes its toll; we arrive at Christmas Day exhausted. Within the context of December busyness, the ancient Christian season of Advent takes on new meaning and acquires renewed importance. May God instill the virtues of *hope*, *peace*, *joy*, *love*, and *faith* in each of us this Advent.

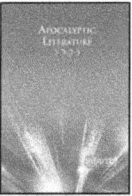

Apocalyptic Literature

This study examines five apocalyptic texts in the Bible—from Zechariah, Daniel, Matthew, and Revelation. With each new year bringing a new prediction of impending doom, it is always a perfect time to get the story straight. Apocalyptic literature does not address the future. It addresses our present.

Approaching a Missional Mindset

The World isn't the same as it once was. We must be the church in a new place, in unimagined ways, and with a wider range of people. Engage your small group with the radical and refreshing challenge of developing a "missional lifestyle."

Baptist Freedom
Celebrating Our Baptist Heritage
What makes a Baptist a Baptist? Of course, the ultimate answer is simple: membership in a local Baptist church. But there are all kinds of Baptist churches! What are the spiritual and theological marks of a Baptist? What is the shape and the feel of Baptist Christianity?

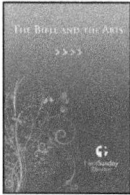

The Bible and the Arts
God has used artistic expression throughout the centuries to convey truth, offer blessing, and urge believers to deeper faithfulness. In modern life, artistic expression flourishes, from movies to books to music to paintings to photographs. Sometimes artists are intentional about trying to portray God's truths. Other times, perhaps God is working even when the artist is unaware of it. As believers, we may hear and see God at work in many art forms.

The Birthday of a King
The first four lessons in this unit draw inspiration from a traditional interpretation of the Advent candles as the Prophets' Candle, the Bethlehem Candle, the Shepherds' Candle, and the Angels' Candle. The final lesson, which occurs after Advent, celebrates the theological meaning of Jesus' birth as described in the prologue to John's Gospel.

Challenges of the Christian Life
The way of the cross is difficult, and taking Jesus seriously means looking honestly at how we fall short of God's best hopes for us and seeing how much we need God's grace. For all of us there are times when we need to remember that Christ is our saving grace and recommit ourselves to the journey of faith, rediscovering, again and again, the life-giving purpose described in the book of Ephesians.

Christ Is Born!
Even in the midst of difficult circumstances, Advent is a time when we can find hope. Much like today, people in the 1st century church faced struggles. Examining the Gospel of Matthew, lessons include "Waiting for Christ," "Preparing for Christ," "Expecting Christ," "Announcing Christ," and "The Arrival of Christ."

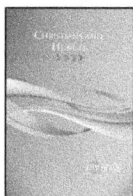

Christians and Hunger

These sessions challenge us to apply gospel lenses and holy imagination to what literally gives us energy to live: food. With God's grace, we have the opportunity to imagine communities where tables are large and all are fed.

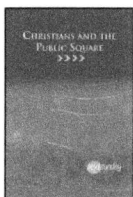

Christians and the Public Square

Politics and faith are tricky areas for Christians to negotiate. The First Amendment to the Constitution guarantees religious freedom for all Americans. As Christians who are also citizens, questions abound: How do we distinguish between faithful and unfaithful forms of civic engagement? How do we give Caesar his due while giving our all to God?

Christmas in Mark

In the early chapters of Mark, we will encounter a Christmas story. This story, however, will not be quite like the one told by other Gospel writers, but it will resonate with the reality of your life. Mark doesn't deny the beauty or reality of the nativity; however, he seems to believe that Christmas begins—the gospel begins—when Christ intrudes upon the hard realities of life.

The Church on a Mission

What does it mean to be a church on a mission? The lesson of Acts 1:8 is that we must simultaneously carry out Christ's mandate at home, in our region, in places that have been our blind spots, and around the world.

Colossians
Living the Faith Faithfully

Paul's letter to the Colossians begins with a high-minded philosophical defense of the faith, but concludes with a collection of extremely practical advice for living by faith. This study addresses the questions many Christians face today, helping them apply Paul's practical advice in their own lives.

Easter Confessions

Easter confession is often found on many different lips in the Gospel of John. When we listen carefully, those ancient confessions still echo into this new millennium.

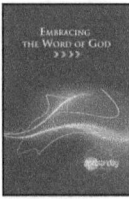

Embracing the Word of God

We live during a time of transition in Christian history. Basic assumptions about the truth of the Christian faith are being questioned, not only by nonbelievers, but by Christians themselves. First John offers a starting point for understanding of what it means to "be" Christian.

Esther: A Woman of Discretion and Valor

The book of Esther is not a record of historical facts as such. Rather, it is a magnificent narrative that refuses to interpret life as being driven by coincidence or happenstance. In the otherwise unknown characters of Esther, Haman, and Mordecai, we trace the movement of the divine hand as God collaborates with God's risk-taking people to rescue them from the hand of their enemies.

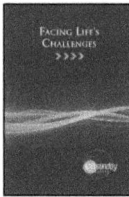

Facing Life's Challenges

This study explores four significant challenges common to most persons of faith: the challenge of new light, the challenge of time's limit, the challenge of living with mystery, and the challenge of authentic spirituality. Although these issues are neither simple nor easy to ponder, this study effectively leads us in confronting these challenges.

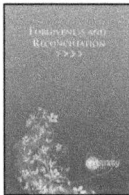

Forgiveness and Reconciliation

Forgiveness is a central issue in our capacity to remain redemptively connected to those relationships we prize. Restoring broken or interrupted relationships is a primary issue for all of us, and managing forgiveness is crucial to the possibility of experiencing reconciliation. Several dimensions of forgiveness affect our lives in significant ways. In this study, we attempt to address a few of those important issues.

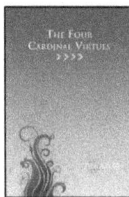

The Four Cardinal Virtues

Christians are learning how to distinguish between members of a church and disciples of Christ. Discipleship involves developing virtues in those who come to our churches seeking life, salvation, grace, mercy. If we want to have something to offer a world in desperate need, then we must return to virtues like discernment, justice, courage, and moderation. We must return to the hard and glorious work of making disciples.

Galatians
Freedom in Christ

Paul wrote with fiery passion, as you will notice from the opening paragraphs of this letter to the Galatians. But his language reveals that he was writing about a crucially important issue—the very nature of salvation in Christ.

Godly Leadership

Nehemiah was called to return to Jerusalem to lead in the sacred task of rebuilding the city's walls. Displaying characteristics often lacking in secular leadership—prayerful humility, a willingness to work with diverse teams, wisdom in confronting conflict, and a passion to stand with the powerless—Nehemiah offered his people a portrait of godly leadership that can still shape our own calls to lead nearly 2,500 years later.

A Holy and Surprising Birth

Christmas begins here—discover these five love stories from the book of Luke and renew your appreciation of God's laborious effort to birth our salvation.

How Does the Church Decide?

An array of decisions draw energy and time from church members. These decisions may be theological, such as mode of baptism, aesthetic, such as the color of the sanctuary carpet, or functional, such as the selection of a new minister. This study will consider how the church has made its decisions in the past to help guide our decisions today.

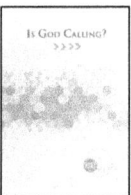

Is God Calling?

Witness the varying forms of God's call, the variety of people called, and the variety of responses. Perhaps God's call to you will become clearer.

James
Gaining True Wisdom
If we'll be honest with God and ourselves as we study what James says, we can make great strides toward wisdom and a living faith.

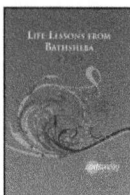

Life Lessons from Bathsheba
Who was Bathsheba? She was a complex figure who developed from the silent object of David's lust into a powerful, vocal, and influential queen mother.

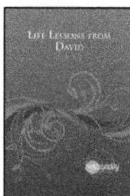

Life Lessons from David
In the Bible, we catch David in the various stages of the human journey: childhood, adolescence, adulthood, and senior adulthood. From the biblical treatment of the stages of David's life, we can land some insights to assist us in better understanding the human journey.

The Matriarchs
The matriarchs of Genesis offer their lives as a testimony of faith, perseverance, and audacity. We learn from their mistakes and suffering. We will gain the hope of Hagar, the joy of Sarah, and the audacity of Rebekah as we are challenged to examine our prejudices and our insecurities while studying Esau and Jacob's wives.

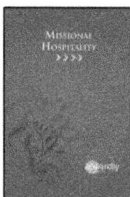

Missional Hospitality
If we are serious about following Jesus, we will be people of open hearts, open hands, and open homes. In other words, as followers of Jesus we will practice the fine art of hospitality. In lesson one, we reflect on hospitality to strangers. In lesson two, we address hospitality to the poor. In lesson three, we focus on hospitality to sinners. In lesson four, we learn about hospitality to newcomers. Lesson five reminds us about our hospitality to Christ.

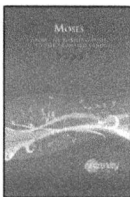

Moses
From the Burning Bush to the Promised Land
We would do well to trace the life of Moses so we might discover how his life changed, both personally and as Israel's leader, as he learned what it meant to love God with all his heart, soul, and strength.

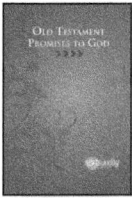

Old Testament Promises to God

Some individuals may feel that our promises couldn't possibly mean anything to God. Perhaps the real question is this: under what circumstances should or do we make such promises? The Old Testament contains several examples of people making promises to God, using the unique form of a biblical "vow."

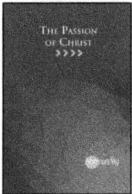

The Passion of Christ

The four lessons in this unit highlight the faith struggles of the early disciples. In lesson one, Jesus addresses the issues of faith and practice. In lesson two, we meet Judas who, like us, struggled with God's Kingdom and human kingdoms. In lesson three, the issue of temptation reminds us that our faith journey is a constant challenge. Lesson Four invites us to remember Peter's experience of "faith failure." Peter's failure, however, is not the final word. There is forgiveness.

The Prayer Life of Jesus

The study of Jesus' prayer life can deepen our own prayer practices. These five sessions examine the importance of prayer at various stages of Jesus' life and ministry. He made no important decisions without consulting God.

Prepare the Way

In these sessions, we will seek to prepare the way toward and into the Christmas season. We begin with the theme of hopeful watchfulness in light of the coming of Christ. Next, we will spend two sessions considering the ministry of John the Baptist, the forerunner of Christ. Then, we will consider Matthew's account of the birth of Jesus and join in wonder at the miracle of "God with us." Finally, we will remember the story of the "holy innocents" killed by Herod in his attempt to eliminate the Christ child's threat to his power.

Proverbs for Living

Long ago, a collection of wise teachers committed themselves to the ways of God and collected this wisdom into what we know as the book of Proverbs. These four lessons explore the simple truth of Proverbs: there is a good life to be had—a life lived in faithfulness to God.

Qualities of Our Missional God

Too often we are tempted to let "numbers" drive missions. The book of Numbers reminds us that missions is motivated by something deeper. Missions reflects the heart and nature of God. If we can just get past the math, we can see God's nature clearly in the book of Numbers. . . in the wilderness.

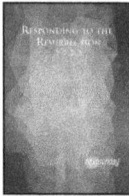

Responding to the Resurrection

All major events of human history elicit responses as varied as the personalities and situations represented by those affected. No one witnesses a world-changing event without being affected in some way. Studying the response of early followers helps us to shape our own response to the resurrection of Jesus. Each of us must consider our response to Jesus' life, teachings, death, resurrection, and call on our lives.

The Seven Deadly Sins

What exactly is sin? Just as we organize our cupboards and our schedules to make sense of our lives, Christian thinkers have organized sin into a number of categories in order to understand and surrender these patterns to God. The notion of "seven deadly sins" emerged as a way to recognize specific dangers to our spiritual lives. The purpose of the book is to guide people away from sin and into a wise and godly life.

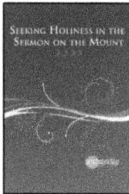

Seeking Holiness in the Sermon on the Mount

The Sermon on the Mount has long been recognized as the pinnacle of Jesus' teaching. But with this importance in mind, it's easy to think of Jesus' teachings as lofty and idealistic, offering little guidance for everyday life. Perhaps Jesus' sermon allows us to see beyond ourselves, beyond our own failures and shortcomings—revealing God's intention for our lives.

Sing We Now of Christmas

In this study, we will explore some familiar prophecies, as well as the Gospel birth narratives, through the lens of five traditional Christmas carols. As carols have grown to be a fuller and more meaningful part of our worship and celebration, so too can the stories of Jesus' birth continue to grow within us and enrich our faith experience.

Spiritual Disciplines
Obligation or Opportunity?

The spiritual disciplines help deepen a believer's faith and increases his or her intimacy with Christ. In this study, we take a deeper look at some of the disciplines and consider their practice as a response to God's love.

Stewardship
A Way of Living

Great News! Stewardship is not about money! At least not *just* about money. Certainly, stewardship relates to money, and, yes, we need to tithe. However, stewardship branches out into multiple areas of life. Properly practiced, this act of service can lead to peace and purpose in living.

The Ten Commandments

When the Ten Commandments are in the news, it is usually because a judge or teacher has hung them up on the walls. The Ten Commandments do not need to be posted or even preached nearly so much as they need to be practiced and viewed as life-giving, joyful affirmations of a better way of life.

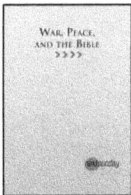

War, Peace, and the Bible

As people of faith, we are faced daily with an expectation that we participate in violent actions, our willingness to allow violence in the world to continue, and our response to violence in our lives. Is there a place for war and violence in our faith?

What Would Jesus Say?
A Lenten Study

To address what Jesus would say, we need to discover what Jesus did say. These lessons will attempt to help us understand Jesus' teachings and apply them today.

The Wonder of Easter

In 1 Corinthians 15, Paul asserts that the message that Jesus died for our sins, was buried, and rose on the third day is "of first importance" (v. 3). It is the core of the gospel story and of the Christian faith. But as much as Easter is a mystery to contemplate, it is also a hope to embrace and good news to proclaim.

**NextSunday Studies
are available from**

NextSunday
Resources

www.ingramcontent.com/pod-product-compliance
Lightning Source LLC
Chambersburg PA
CBHW070541030426
42337CB00016B/2303